Waiting for Mr. Right

Book 1: Mr. Right Series

by

Barbara Precourt

with

Lisa Raftery

First published by Dog Ear Publishing
4010 W 86th Street, Ste H
Indianapolis, IN 46268
www.dogearpublishing.net

ISBN: 978-160844-032-0

This book is a work of fiction. Places, events, and situations in this
book are purely fictional and any resemblance to actual persons,
living or dead, is coincidental.

This paper is acid free and meets all ANSI standards
for archival quality paper.
Printed in the United States of America

Endorsements

This book chronicles the charming tale of an adolescent woman's emergence into adulthood. The trials that Julia encounters throughout her journey spotlight many of the issues that teenagers face. This book provides young women with appropriate role models and problem-solving strategies for dealing with those issues. Additionally, parents can use Julia's life struggles to initiate meaningful, non-threatening conversations with their daughters concerning their own lives. I highly recommend this book to both young women and parents alike. Enjoy!

Melissa Hurst, P.sy.D.
Doctor of Clinical Psychology

I loved this book! It kept me riveted until the end. I can't wait until my own granddaughters are old enough to read it. In fact, I think every woman should read this—whether she's a daughter, mother, or grandmother. It has all the components of an exciting novel with great insights into what young women are currently facing in their lives. The character issues and life applications are priceless. I highly endorse this book.

Trudi Blount
Seminar Leader and International Speaker
Ken Blount Ministries

This book is a must-read for teenage girls! Julia's experience clearly illustrates the danger that comes from moving out from what you know is right. I pray that every young woman who reads this realizes the safety and great benefit of staying in the light of God's Word and His ways.

Pastor Victoria Raftery
Laurel Church Ministries

Dedication

Waiting for Mr. Right is dedicated to my daughter, Lisa, who has been a constant source of joy and blessing in my life. Seeing her safely delivered in marriage to her Mr. Right has been the fulfillment of a mother's prayers and a young girl's dreams.

Acknowledgements

I want to extend my deepest gratitude to the following people who helped make this book possible:

My daughter, Lisa Raftery, who is now in full-time ministry with her husband, Eric Shawn Raftery, founder of LifeRaft. Lisa served as my editor and *tirelessly* collaborated with me on every page of the **Mr. Right Series**, *Waiting for Mr. Right* being the first book. Her years of ministry experience and counseling with young women have greatly contributed to the quality of this work.

My son, Jeff Precourt, who opened my eyes to the need for such a book to help girls make better choices in their dating relationships

Lindsay Russo, for her excellent cover design

Kim Sgouroudis, who helped with some of the editing

My daughter-in-law, Stephanie Precourt, for her enthusiastic support and practical input

Roger Precourt, my Mr. Right, who let me spend an inordinate number of hours in front of my computer, writing

Pastors Larry and Victoria Raftery for all their encouragement and intercession regarding this work

Most importantly, to the Holy Spirit, for allowing me to serve as His scribe and communicate the Father's heart to young ladies who desperately need to pursue Him as their *first* love

Contents

Chapter 1

Unexpected Turn

I had always loved fairy tales as a girl; *Sleeping Beauty* was my favorite. The princess in that story was hidden away for safety, and like her, I felt that I was overprotected. I used to fantasize about a handsome prince that would someday come and rescue me from *my* life of isolation.

You see, growing up as a Christian, I felt my parents were way too strict. Even though I knew it was because they loved me, when I got into high school, I began to resent some of their restrictions. I'd accepted Jesus as my Savior and wanted to serve God, but I felt like other girls my age were having much more fun than I was. They had dates, bought pretty dresses for dances, and were always talking about their boyfriends. I secretly wanted all of those experiences, too.

Since my parents wouldn't let me date or go to dances, I read novels by the dozens and watched lots of romantic movies. Even though the things I read and watched were clean and innocent, I was spending far too much time thinking about being in love.

When I first arrived at Tyler University, I was as excited as any freshman, with high hopes for my college experience. While things did go well for me academically the first semester, my social life was a big zero. I'd found a good church to attend, but I still missed my friends from home.

Eventually, a girl from one of my classes invited me to join a Christian group on campus. I jumped at the chance hoping to meet some Christian guys there. To my disappointment, the few that I would've been interested in dating already had girlfriends. With no romantic prospects in sight, attending the meetings gave me the same *let's-go-to-youth-group* feeling I'd had in high school. After a while, it felt like I was the only one who didn't have a boyfriend. "Why isn't it happening for me?" I would think, doubting myself.

In the weeks that followed, my fears and frustrations started to depress me, causing my spiritual life to suffer. I rarely felt like reading my Bible anymore. When I did force myself, I was only going through the motions, not getting much out of what I was reading. Praying felt just as meaningless since all I did was complain anyway.

It was almost the end of the first semester before things took an unexpected turn. One day a girl in my English class motioned to me and silently passed over an envelope. Surprised, I took it from her and opened it. It was an invitation to join the most popular sorority on campus—one with a reputation for partying.

Immediately, there was a check in my spirit, a warning that said, "This would be a mistake. Don't even think about it!" I agreed with that first impression, but it still felt good to be asked. Sliding the envelope into my English book, I returned my attention to the professor's lecture and continued taking notes.

I forgot all about it until the next day when Theresa showed up at my dorm room. "Hey, Julia. I just came by to check on the invite I gave you yesterday."

I was about to say that I wasn't interested in the sorority when she added, "Trust me; you want to pledge. Our girls are the first ones invited to all the dances on campus. We go to a lot of great parties, too. I know you're sort of a Miss Religious, but honestly, we don't do anything bad, and you'll get to meet tons of guys. If you don't join, you'll spend all your weekends alone up here in this room. It's up to you. All decisions have to be made by Friday night," she announced before breezing out the door.

After she left, I felt uneasy. Saying *no* was clearly the right choice for me, but my mind was at war with my spirit. The thought of another boring semester was more than I could bear. I knew I should read my Bible and pray until I felt peace, but I stubbornly resisted that idea.

I should have discussed joining the sorority with my Christian group on Thursday night, but once I was there, it never seemed the right time to bring up the subject. Maybe I was just afraid they would tell me not to pledge. Either way, I never talked to them about it. By Friday, my mind had won the battle. I ended up going to the meeting at the sorority and agreeing to pledge.

Once I was back in my dorm room, I had a chance to think about the choice I'd just made. I didn't feel good about it, but there was no turning back. It was something I really wanted to do.

Pulling this off wasn't going to be easy, but I was confident I could do it. Since I couldn't tell my parents I was moving into a sorority house, I'd have to find ways to get my mail and phone calls relayed to me from the dorm. My roommate and I got along pretty well; I was sure she would coop-erate. College life was hectic, so I could simply make up an excuse for never being in my room when my mom or dad called. They usually called me on my cell phone anyway, and that would al-ways be with me.

I had the financial part figured out as well. My dad gave me money for my tuition, dorm payment, and expenses by the semester; I handled paying it all. Since living at the sorority house was only a little more than at the dorm, my parents would never know about the switch. I wasn't worried about unexpected visits from them either. The campus was an eight-hour drive from my house, and I had my own car at school to drive home for holidays. Besides, my parents trusted me; they wouldn't suspect a thing.

What I was doing was totally out of character for me, but I rationalized that I needed time to prove that I could go to parties and dances, have fun like other girls, and still be a good Christian witness at the same time. After all, God could use me at the sorority house to lead girls to Christ, couldn't He? I felt like this was my one chance to be free.

At first, everything seemed fine. Being a sorority pledge was exciting, and I began meeting a whole new set of people. Before long, I was accepted and moved into the sorority house my second semester. I got all the help I needed moving my things from some guys in a nearby fraternity. They all seemed nice, and I worked hard at convincing myself that what I was doing was not a compromise, just a chance to share Christ with others. I promised myself that I would *not* get romantically involved with any guy who wasn't a Christian.

Our sorority house was a huge, Victorian mansion. Built by an affluent family generations before, it had been donated to the university and designated for our sorority chapter. Our housemother was in her late sixties, a lifelong friend to the previous, and now deceased, owners. Very strict, prim, and proper, she was like someone out of another era.

The front sitting room of the mansion had a brass plaque at the doorway that read *The Parlor.* Our housemother referred to male students as *gen-*

tlemen callers, and they were only allowed in the parlor. No guys could go up to our rooms.

My room on the second floor was much nicer than the one I'd had at the dorm. It was a little bigger with its own bathroom connecting to the room next door. My roommate, Fran, was friendly and full of energy. I was hopeful that we would have a great semester together.

After all my things were organized and put away, I fell into bed, exhausted. Fran was already sound asleep. As I lay there surveying my new surroundings, listening to unfamiliar sounds, my heart felt a little homesick. But that feeling subsided as I slipped into a deep sleep, unaware that I was gradually moving out of the light and into a darkness that would seek to destroy me.

Chapter 2

Mr. Wonderful

The morning sunshine forced its way through a partially-open window shade, disrupting my peaceful sleep and thrusting me into a completely new world—sorority life. Theresa took it upon herself to be my personal social director, making sure I knew about every upcoming event.

The first party I went to was at another student's apartment. Even though there were some good-looking guys there, I concentrated on staying close to the girls I knew, keeping my conversations with the guys casual. It was pretty obvious that they weren't Christians, but since I didn't intend to date any of them, it wasn't a problem.

There was always some smoking and drinking at the parties I attended, but it wasn't until I went to my first frat party that I saw the kind of drinking my parents had always warned me about. Beer was flowing like a river, and almost everyone was carrying a drink in his or her hand. Even girls from my sorority were losing control and getting drunk. I heard one of them say that the hard stuff was being served in the kitchen.

The noise level was increasing by the minute, both from the CDs that were blaring from the stereo and the shouts of those who were already drunk and trying to be heard over the deafening music. As I stood there exchanging small talk with a few girls, I secretly asked myself, "What am I doing here?"

After a while, I excused myself to go to the bathroom but headed for the back door instead. I had only made it about halfway when some guy grabbed my arm and pulled me down into a chair with him. He was obviously very drunk. After a brief struggle, I pulled free from him and continued my escape. Once outside, I ran back to the sorority house and headed straight for my room.

By then it was almost midnight. As I passed by one of the rooms in my hallway, I heard a girl sobbing. Seeing that the door was ajar, I pushed it open just enough to peek my head inside. Lying on the bed was Gretchen, one of the most popular girls in our sorority.

I had seen her at the party earlier and was surprised she was back in her room this early. All I really knew about Gretchen was that she had a good-looking boyfriend she'd been dating for almost two years. The way she was crying, I figured they must have had a fight.

Her roommate was still out, so I decided to go in and try to console her. Closing the door behind me, I softly called out her name and asked if I could come in. Gretchen pushed herself up on the bed and motioned for me to come sit beside her. Once I sat down, she began pouring her heart out to me. She told me that she and her boyfriend were sleeping together—that she'd gotten pregnant the previous year and he had arranged for her to have an abortion.

"I've never gotten over the guilt," she admitted, "and he still wants to have sex without a condom. I don't want to because I'm afraid I'll get pregnant again. I'm on the pill, but I was taking it last year and still got pregnant. We fought about it again tonight. He said he's sick of our whole relationship, and we broke up."

Gretchen eventually cried herself to sleep. I covered her with a blanket before quietly leaving for my room. Even though I felt sad for Gretchen and what she was facing, I couldn't help but wonder where my own life was going.

I never told anyone about my conversation with Gretchen. She naturally felt awkward after confiding in me that night, so she managed to avoid me whenever she could. She and Brad were back together in three days. I assumed that meant she was willing to continue the relationship on his terms.

Meanwhile, disturbing reports were circulating around the house on a regular basis. We heard that one girl on the first floor tested HIV positive, while another girl found out that her boyfriend had gotten someone else pregnant. There were incidents of date rape and drunken girls getting picked up by the police almost every weekend.

Was this the freedom I thought I'd missed out on as a Christian? *No thanks!* All I wanted was to make it through the next few months and get back to the dorm when school started up again in the fall.

I had hoped to keep a low profile while still at the sorority house, but the girls kept pressuring me to attend every social event that came along. Furthermore, my roommate, Fran, was determined to find me a boyfriend. She'd been dating a guy named J.R. for several months. He was as quiet and reserved as she was uninhibited and crazy.

J.R. lived in one of the frat houses on the edge of campus. His roommate told him he wanted to meet me. When Fran heard that, she started to work on me, trying to get me to go out with him. But I had seen firsthand what guys from the fraternities were like and wanted nothing to do with them.

I tried explaining to her that I didn't want to date any guy who wasn't a committed Christian. She couldn't understand why, saying, "I'm not asking you to *marry* the man, Julia. Just go out on a date with him." No matter how many times she asked me about it, my emphatic *no* never discouraged her. Each day gave her renewed hope that she could break me down.

Since joining the sorority, I had let my attendance slip at church and with my Bible study group. I knew I needed to recommit to both. Although it was awkward at first, I felt like I was at least taking the first steps to getting my spiritual life back in order. Everyone from my study group seemed glad to have me back, but I still felt uncomfortable since they knew I had joined the sorority.

Meanwhile, I immersed myself in my studies. The campus library became my new home when I wasn't sleeping or in classes. I could work there without being bombarded with questions about my social life. It was also a good place to hide from Fran and her incessant nagging about going out with J.R.'s roommate.

Eventually, I found another little hideout. It was a campus café called The Coffee Cup, located about two blocks from the library. I would often stop by there to talk with a girl from my Bible study group. Karen and I were both hooked on cappuccino. Fran never came in, but J.R. did, usually to get something for takeout. Fortunately, he was always in a hurry and didn't have time to bug me about meeting his friend.

My hours at the library started to increase because of a paper that was almost due. I dedicated one whole afternoon to finishing it and became so engrossed in my work that I lost track of time. When I glanced up at the clock, I saw that I had already missed the first half of my Bible study. Being more than ready to quit for the day, I stuffed my books into my backpack and walked down to The Coffee Cup instead.

When I arrived, I got something to drink and then plopped down at a table in the back. Sipping my cappuccino, I began reviewing the paper I had just finished. Deep in concentration, it startled me when a voice asked, "Do you mind if I sit here?"

Looking up, I saw that there were plenty of other seats available. This guy had evidently caught me off guard because I heard myself tell him it was fine. Before he sat down, I was able to quickly look him over. He was about six feet tall, well-built, and very handsome.

"My name's Jay," he said, sliding into the seat across from me. Before I could respond, he added, "And you're Julia."

My face must have shown my surprise because he asked the obvious question in my mind. "And you're wondering how I already know your name, right?"

"Right," I shyly replied.

"Actually, I've known it for a while. I saw you over a month ago at a frat party down the street from your sorority house. I was there that night, too. When I saw you across the room, I asked around and found out your name and what sorority you were from.

"I think I noticed you because you seemed as bored as I was there. I started to come over and introduce myself, but I lost sight of you. When I finally found you, I could see that some guy had you pinned down in a chair. I was on my way to rescue you, but by the time I got there, you had disappeared again. Do you believe in fate?" he asked, smiling.

I told him I didn't.

"Well, maybe I can change your mind. When you disappeared, I felt like the prince left with the glass slipper and no girl. But at least I knew where you lived. I went home that night and told my roommate about seeing you. He started laughing when he heard your name because he already knows you." Suddenly, I realized he was talking about J.R., and I could feel my face turning red.

"Don't you know how hard it is on a guy to be rejected over and over? I've been trying to meet you for weeks, and all I keep hearing is how you're not interested. J.R. told me you stop in here a lot, so I've been keeping an eye out for you. Every time I see you, though, you're with one of your friends. Since you were alone tonight, I decided to take a chance and introduce myself. So, am I as scary as you thought I'd be?"

I couldn't help but laugh, partly because of what he had said and partly because I was embarrassed. I had repeatedly refused to go out with this guy under any circumstances; now here he was, sitting across the table from me. So this was the Jason Wells that Fran had been pressuring me to meet. What was I going to say to him? I could see that he was not going to speak next. He just sat there smiling at me, waiting for a response.

Finally, I attempted to explain. "I never said anything like that. I just told Fran I didn't want to go out with any guy that wasn't a Christian."

"How did you know I wasn't a Christian?" he asked, amused.

"Because I haven't met one guy from the frat houses that thinks of Jesus as anything more than a swear word."

"Okay, so you're saying that if a guy belongs to a fraternity, he can't be a Christian. But you're a Christian, and you're in a sorority."

He had me there; now I was totally out of ammunition.

"You don't have an answer for that one, do you?" he laughed. "For your information, I've gone to church all my life, and I'm a great Christian guy. Now that we've got that settled, will you *please* go out with me this weekend?" His charm persuaded me to yield. Sheepishly, I consented with a smile and a nod.

That first meeting ended my daily visits to the library. When I wasn't in class, I was with Jay. He was definitely Mr. Wonderful. We had fun no matter what we were doing: We studied together, he went to church with me, and The Coffee Cup became our favorite place to meet between classes.

Jay had a Thursday night class, so he couldn't go with me to my Bible study group. He had deliberately cut class the night we met for the first time because he wanted to talk to me alone. Fran and J. R. were wearing out the phrase *I told you so*, but I didn't care. I was in love, and my senses and emotions were in a whirl. I wasn't thinking anymore, just feeling—and being in love felt good.

Chapter 3

Failed Attempt

After about a month of dating Jay, I started to notice a change in our relationship; he was becoming much more passionate when we were kissing good night. Up until then, he had always been a perfect gentleman. But after I told him how much I loved him, he seemed to want to express his feelings for me more and more physically. He looked for opportunities for us to be alone so he could hold and kiss me for longer periods of time. He often tried to French kiss me, and his hands began to wander.

I repeatedly explained to Jay that I was a virgin and wouldn't go any further with him than light kissing. He always said he was sorry when he pushed for more, blaming it on loving me so much. I accepted his apologies with the hope that he would change, but he didn't. The passion he felt for me increased with every date, and having to monitor his every touch made it impossible for me to relax in his embrace anymore. Before long I began to feel fear, instead of love, for Jay.

As my fears grew, I needed to talk to someone and get some advice. I wanted to call Karen, but we hadn't been that close lately. Besides, having bragged so much to her about Jay, I was embarrassed to say anything. Fran and I were pretty good friends, yet I didn't want to share something this personal with her, especially since her boyfriend was Jay's roommate. Not seeing any other option, I decided to deal with the problem myself.

I was able to keep Jay's passion for me under control until one Saturday night. We had just driven back from seeing a movie and were parked behind my sorority house, talking. Jay turned off the motor, flipped up the armrest, and pulled me close to him. Leaning down, he started to kiss me. I tensed up a little at first, wondering if I'd have to keep him in line, as usual. But he was so tender and gentle this time that I began to relax.

After we had been kissing for a while, I sensed that he was starting to lose it. Suddenly, he was all over me, and I heard my blouse rip as I tried to push his hands away. By then he was already on top of me, pinning me down in the front seat.

"I want you, Julia, right now!" he demanded.

"Stop, Jay!" I cried over and over as I struggled beneath him.

He never heard me. I no longer mattered to him as a person—all he cared about was getting what he wanted. My screams must have been loud enough to draw some attention because the door opened on my side of the car.

"What's going on in there?" a male voice shouted. That was the diversion I needed. Startled,

Jay raised up and relaxed his grip long enough for me to pull free and scramble out of the car. My rescuers turned out to be a girl from the first floor and her boyfriend. Still frightened, I didn't take time to say thanks. I just pushed past them and escaped into the sorority house.

I managed to keep my composure until I reached my room. Seeing that Fran was still out, I burst into tears. I was still crying when my cell phone rang. It was Jay. "I'm so sorry, Julia. Please forgive me," he begged.

"No more, Jay!" I snapped angrily. "We're through. Don't ever call me again!"

Shaking, I quickly turned off my phone. No doubt Jay would keep calling, but I didn't care. I knew the awful truth: Jay wasn't a Christian at all. He had just said that he was to get me to date him.

I was still trembling when I crawled into bed. Until that night, I'd never experienced the strength a man can exert over a woman. Jay had overpowered me in his car, and if Sarah and her boyfriend hadn't opened the door, I would've been the next date-rape victim on campus.

I remembered the time I'd comforted Gretchen in her room. There was no one to comfort me. I had cut myself off from a truthful relationship with my parents and Christian friends, leaving me alone to deal with all the hurt and anxiety I was feeling. That night I was the one who cried myself to sleep.

When I awoke the next morning, I told Fran about what had happened the night before with Jay and my decision to break it off with him. She agreed that Jay had no right to push himself on me, but I got the feeling she thought I was overreacting. I had suspected for some time that Fran and J.R. were sleeping together. Maybe that was why she couldn't understand how important my virginity was to me.

When the two girls in the adjoining room heard that Jay and I had broken up, they begged me to give him another chance. Even though I told them what Jay had done, they were convinced that he wasn't really a bad guy. Jay was handsome and charming; all the girls in my sorority liked him. But I didn't care. I knew the real Jay and wanted nothing more to do with him. I had broken up with him over the phone the night before, thinking it was all over between us. I would soon find out that I was wrong.

Because I didn't feel like seeing anyone the next day, I stayed home from church and tried to catch up on some of the studies I'd been neglecting lately. While I was reading, I remembered that I'd turned off my cell. Turning it back on, I listened to my voicemail.

I figured Jay would be on there repeatedly, but I needed to check and see if Toni had called from the dorm with a message from my parents. The first ten messages were from Jay, begging me to call him, to forgive him, to meet him. The last one was from Toni with instructions to call my mom *immediately*.

Momentarily, I forgot all about my troubles with Jay and began to stress over Toni's message. Had my parents started to suspect something? Was I in trouble with them? Had something gone wrong at home? My imagination was running wild. I started to phone my mom right away, but saw that it was too early. My parents were still at church. I'd have to wait at least another hour to make the call.

As I sat on my bed deleting all of Jay's messages, my phone suddenly rang. I answered it without checking the caller ID, panicked that Toni was calling with another message from my mom. It was Jay.

"Julia, please don't hang up!" he pleaded. "We need to talk. Let me come over and pick you up."

My heart was pounding, but I knew I had to pull myself together and make my position clear to him one last time. "We're finished, Jay. We don't have anything to talk about. I don't ever want to be alone with you again. I saw the real you last night. I want out! You'll just have to accept that. Stop calling me!"

"I love you so much, Julia, and I know you still love me. I can't let you go."

"Think about what happened last night, Jay. You would've raped me right there in your car if Sarah and her boyfriend hadn't stopped you!"

"You're exaggerating, Julia," he accused. "I admit I acted like a jerk last night. I don't blame you for being mad. But I promise it'll never happen again."

"I don't believe you, Jay. Don't call me anymore!" I demanded before hanging up and tossing my phone to the end of the bed. I couldn't turn it off again in case Toni called, but I would certainly check my caller ID each time it rang now.

I managed to get some reading done until it was time to make my call home. Slowly dialing the number, I held my breath until my dad answered on the second ring. Hearing his voice almost made me burst into tears and tell all, but I restrained myself and greeted him with my usual, "Hey, Dad."

"That you, sweetheart?"

"Yes. Is anything wrong? Mom left a message for me to call immediately..."

"She's right here," he said. "Let's ask her."

My mom's was the next voice I heard. "Are you okay, Julia?"

"Of course, Mom. Why?"

She sounded concerned. "I don't know, honey. I guess it's a lot of things. When I can't reach you on your cell and I try you at the dorm, you're never there. Even when it's really late. And when I pray for you lately, I have an uneasiness in my spirit. I'm sensing that something's wrong. If you're having a problem at school, please tell us so we can help you."

I couldn't bring myself to tell her the truth, so I tried to come up with an acceptable answer.

"That's just your imagination working on you, Mom. Everything's fine."

I knew she wasn't convinced when she persisted further. "There isn't anything you can't share with us, Julia. Remember that we love you and always will. You can count on us to be there for you, no matter what."

"Thanks, Mom. But don't worry; everything's great." Feeling pressured, I lied to get off the phone. "I've got to go now. Some girls are waiting for me to go out for lunch. I'll be coming home for spring break next week. We'll have lots of time to talk then."

As I ended the call, I felt both relief and guilt sweep over me. When you're this far into doing what you know is wrong, you're no longer thinking clearly. Your whole life is a lie, and you feel threatened by people who are still walking in the truth. It sounds silly, but you're actually afraid of them. Pride causes you to try to fix things on your own so you can save face and get back to where you should be without anyone knowing how foolish you've been.

In my mind, all I had to do was get through the semester. Jay was graduating in the spring, and he had already accepted a job in another state. Next term I would be back in the dorm, Jay would be gone, and his failed attempt to rape me would be a distant memory. My parents would never have to know.

The next week was a challenge since I had two exams and a paper due before leaving for home on Friday. To make things worse, Jay continued to leave dozens of voicemail and text messages on my phone. He even dropped off several notes at the sorority house. All had the same request: *please let me see you!*

I managed to avoid him during the day by slipping in and out of side and back entrances and even skipping some classes. Most of the time, I stayed my room. I felt like a prisoner, but it was the only place I felt safe. He showed up at the sorority house a couple of times asking to see me, but I refused to leave my room and come down.

It seemed like forever, but Thursday evening finally arrived. After dinner in my room, I packed my things and set them by the door. Fran was out somewhere with J.R., as always. I went to bed early, wanting to get some rest before the long drive ahead of me the next day. I planned to get on the road as soon as it was light.

Spending a whole week at home would be heaven—mainly because I'd no longer be looking over my shoulder every minute trying to avoid Jay. It was going to be nice to relax for a change. Once he had some time totally away from me, I was sure that Jay would settle down and give up the pursuit.

The drive home went well. I listened to music and drank in the beauty of the scenery around me. Trees that had been barren all winter were coming alive with their greenery; bright yellow daffodils were beginning to bloom. Spring was in the air with a promise of better days to come.

Once home, I began to feel more like myself again. While I was there, I realized just how good everything had always been for me. The house itself seemed warmer, the food tasted better, and even my bed felt more comfortable. Spending time with my parents was sweeter, too. I felt their love reaching out to me stronger than ever, their hugs and kisses healing wounds they couldn't see.

Hearing my pastor preach on Sunday was great, and I had fun going out with my Christian friends during the week. I didn't want my vacation to end, but all too soon, it was time to go back to school. At least I'd done a good job of acting while I was home, convincing my parents that everything at Tyler was going well.

As usual, my parents prayed with me by the door before I left to go back to campus. When my mom hugged me goodbye, she whispered in my ear, "You're going to have to tell me sooner or later, Julia. When you're ready, you know where I am." Neither of us said anything more.

The drive back was not as pleasant as the trip home had been. My mom's words kept ringing in my ears. She knew me like no one else; I resented not being able to fool her. Even though she was sensing something, she still didn't know anything concrete, and I was determined to handle the few weeks I had left at school without my parents' help. I just couldn't let them know how badly I had messed up the first time I was free to make my own choices. Besides, Jay had been given a whole week to calm down over break. I convinced myself that he'd finally given up on me.

Refusing to think about him another second, I popped in my favorite CD and sang along to lift my spirits. At the time, I had no way of knowing that I was driving back into a series of events I would not soon forget.

Chapter 4

Facing the Problem

I pulled into the circular drive of the sorority house just before dark and unloaded my bags on the sidewalk. Some other girls were returning at the same time, each making a neat pile similar to mine. One of them watched our things while the rest of us parked our cars alongside the building.

Returning to the front, we picked up our respective pieces of luggage and attempted to get everything up the stairs and into the building. Dropping things and bumping into one another on the way in, we were all laughing as we squeezed through the front door. Suddenly, I felt someone from behind take my largest bag. When I turned around, I was looking directly into Jay's face.

"Welcome back, beautiful," he said with a smile as though nothing had happened. "I've been waiting for you."

When I saw him, I panicked, dropped everything in my arms, and ran. My first instinct was to get to my room, but there wasn't enough time to get away from him. After taking just a few steps, Jay caught my arm and jerked me around.

"Why are you acting like this?" he shouted, attracting everyone's attention. By this time, I was crying hysterically. The harder I tried to pull away from him, the stronger his grip became. "I'm not going to let go of you, so you may as well calm down and listen to me," he insisted.

There were several girls still in the lobby, probably stalling to see what would happen next. Since there were people around, I decided it was safe to just talk to Jay. Trying to compose myself, I wiped away some tears with my hand and took a couple of deep breaths. Once I'd stopped crying, he led me over to a nearby couch in the parlor, and we sat down.

Releasing his hold on my arm, he said, "I never meant to hurt you that night, Julia. You've got to believe me. You're everything I want in a girl; I don't want to lose you. I've admitted I was wrong and apologized over and over. What else can I do to make things right?"

He did seem truly sorry. When I looked into his eyes, I caught a glimpse of the Jay I had dated those first few weeks. Momentarily, my emotions relived how it felt to love him. But that only lasted for a second as I remembered all the times we were together afterwards and how it felt to fear him, especially that last Saturday night.

"You're at least looking at me again," Jay stated, interrupting my thoughts. "But you haven't answered my question yet. How can I make things right between us?"

"You can't, Jay. Things weren't right from the start. I told you then I couldn't date a guy that wasn't a Christian."

"Not again!" Jay exclaimed, apparently hurt. "I thought we settled my Christian status a long time ago."

"Not really. I wanted to believe you were a Christian so I could have a boyfriend. But now I know that you don't have a relationship with God."

"How could you know that? Are you psychic or something?"

I shocked Jay with my answer. "*You* told me when I spent time with you. You never talked about Jesus or spiritual things when we were together. Even when we went to church, you didn't seem all that interested in what was going on. I knew in my heart that something was wrong, but I didn't want to believe it. You were the one who *made* me believe it when you kept pushing me past the boundaries I'd set.

"A Christian guy would've respected my virginity and understood my right to remain pure until my wedding night. You didn't. In fact, you almost *took* it from me, Jay! Virginity as a gift you save for the person you marry. It's a beautiful gift because it can only be given once, to one person, and it's not to be given until your wedding night. I don't expect you to understand what I'm saying, but you've got to know that I'm *not* going to date you again. I'm going to wait for a guy who does understand and who's saving himself for me."

I tried to read Jay's response, but he wouldn't look at me. Finally, he painfully asked, "So, what happens to me now? What do I do now that I love you?"

His words pierced my heart. As a non-Christian, he had simply noticed me and asked me out. I, on the other hand, knew better than to date someone without the same level of spiritual commitment. But I hadn't been willing to wait and find out where Jay really stood before dating him. My selfishness and immaturity were now causing him a lot of pain—pain that could have easily been avoided. The answer I gave him was the only one I could.

"In time your feelings for me will go away. Please forgive me for hurting you." With that I stood up and walked out of the parlor. This time, Jay didn't try to stop me. Quietly gathering up my luggage from the lobby, I carried it upstairs to my room.

When I walked through the door, I saw Fran's things tossed here and there. Apparently, she was back from break and out with J.R. again. I called my parents right away to let them know I had made it back to school safely. Then I unpacked.

Even though I still felt guilty about Jay, things between us were finally resolved, and I was glad. Facing the problem is not always pleasant, but it needs to be done. "Only seven more weeks of school and my secret life will be over," I murmured to myself.

I was still awake in bed when Fran came in that night, but I pretended to be asleep already. I didn't want to talk about what had happened earlier with Jay, knowing that, in her eyes, I was the bad guy in the relationship. A confrontation was inevitable, but at least I could put it off for a few more hours.

The next morning I was already showered and dressed for my early class before Fran awoke. As I quietly inserted some folders into my backpack, Fran's morning voice weakly made its way across the room. "I saw Jay last night after you got through with him. He came back to the frat house looking like he'd taken a real beating. Honestly, Julia, this guy's in love with you. You're crazy if you dump him like this."

I didn't have time to defend myself. It wouldn't have done any good anyway, so I merely answered, "I'm not asking you to agree with me, Fran." That said, I picked up my backpack and left.

Outside, the morning air was crisp and cool. It felt good to walk off my frustration. I knew I had to somehow establish a routine and get my mind back on my schoolwork. Dating Jay had been my main focus the last couple of months, but that was over, and I would have to adjust to being alone again.

For the next three days, I was quizzed by almost every girl in the house about the incident in the lobby with Jay. Just as I had anticipated, they all sympathized with him. I think Fran was spreading the word about how much he was hurting. That made me out to be the villain.

One night I went to Theresa's room to borrow a sweater from her. When I walked in, there were at least six girls congregating around her bed. By the hush that fell over the group, I knew they had been talking about me.

The silence was finally broken when Carrie looked at me and asked, "Heard from Jay lately?" The girls all laughed. A few of them had been down in the parlor when Jay grabbed me. They thought that the way he was fighting to keep the girl he loved was so romantic. He had become some kind of hero to them.

Suddenly, I was barraged with comments like "Maybe Jay has learned his lesson," or "Maybe you should give the guy another chance," or "Maybe you just need to grow up." Disgusted, I turned to leave the room without even explaining why I'd come there in the first place. Then, from behind me, I heard someone say, "Or maybe Julia's just smarter than all of us put together."

Looking back to see who had come to my defense, I was shocked to find it was Gretchen. Her statement delivered, she got up, brushed past me, and made her way out the door. I stood there stunned for a few seconds before turning to leave

Theresa's room as well. After that little encounter, I could see the library in my future once again. It would be a much friendlier environment.

The next night, I went to my Thursday Bible study group. Afterwards, Karen and I stopped by The Coffee Cup, where I told her all about Jay and what had happened. She was relieved that I had broken things off with him. Even though Jay had never gone to my Bible study with me, I had talked about him in our discussion groups, saying how happy I was to have a Christian boyfriend. Gary, the leader of our group, knew Jay and was worried about me dating him. He had shared his concern with the rest of the group, and they had all been praying for me for over two months.

Before we left the café, Karen mentioned that she was looking for a new church to attend. She had wanted to try mine for some time, but she knew that Jay and I were going together every Sunday and hadn't wanted to tag along. We agreed that she would be joining me from then on.

To my relief, I got through the next week without a call or text from Jay. Hopeful that he'd finally given up on us, I began to feel more relaxed walking around campus. It wasn't until Saturday that we eventually ran into each other. I was on my way into the library just as he was leaving, and we met on the stairs. Jay smiled and silently walked past me. Then, as I reached for the door, he called out my name. I turned to see him just a few steps below where I stood.

"I'm kind of in a hurry, Jay," I answered awkwardly.

"This won't take long," he promised. "I've been thinking about what you said to me the other day. Maybe I do need to reexamine my beliefs in God. I went to church with my parents when I lived at home, but I got away from going when I came to college. You were the one who got me started again. I need to figure out where I'm at with God, and I really like the services at your church. Is it okay with you if I still go there on Sundays?"

That was the last thing I expected him to ask me. Glad that he wanted to go to church without me as the incentive, I responded, "Of course, Jay. You can go there anytime you want."

"Thanks, Julia. That means a lot," he said gratefully, slipping his backpack onto his shoulder. As I watched him turn and go, I couldn't help but sigh, wondering how long it would take for the empty feeling inside of me to go away.

Chapter 5

A Brand New Deal

Startled by an annoying beeping, I quickly reached over and shut off my alarm. My body was crying out for more sleep, but I had to get up and start getting ready for church. Fran was still unconscious from her late night with J.R., which spared me another debate about Jay.

I picked up Karen right at nine-thirty so I could introduce her to my pastor before the service started. As planned, we arrived at church several minutes early. When the introductions were over, Pastor Scott looked around and asked, "So, where's your boyfriend today?" He could tell from my expression that he had asked the wrong question.

"We're not dating anymore," I answered, embarrassed. "I found out Jay wasn't really a Christian, and I felt we needed to end our relationship."

Before Pastor could reply, he noticed Jay entering the back of the sanctuary. "We'll talk later," he whispered. Karen and I caught a glimpse of Jay as we took our seats in a pew near the front. He found a place to sit somewhere behind us.

The message was good that morning, but I had trouble concentrating on it. Jay's presence was making me uneasy. I couldn't help but question his real motive for coming.

As Pastor was finishing his sermon, I started to feel anxious about facing Jay. My hands grew wet and clammy, and I felt sick to my stomach. Before long, the congregation was invited to stand for the closing prayer. Then we were dismissed.

Not sure what to do, I nervously introduced Karen to a few of the people who had been sitting by us. While we stood talking, Jay walked past us and headed for the front of the church. Seizing the moment, I grabbed Karen's arm and pulled her to the back of the sanctuary. Just before we hurried out the door, curiosity forced me to look back and see where Jay had gone. Oddly enough, he was still up front, standing in line to talk to Pastor Scott.

Hungry after the service, Karen and I stopped at a nearby restaurant for lunch. While we were being served, I noticed Pastor Scott walk through the front door with his family. As they passed by our table, he stopped to talk to us. "So, where's the fire? You girls left in such a rush after service today."

"That was my fault," I confessed. "I wanted to get out of there before Jay had a chance to corner me."

"Actually, it was me he cornered," Pastor Scott replied with a chuckle. "It was right for you to stop dating Jay if you felt his spiritual life wasn't right, Julia. But after my talk with him today, I can tell you he's asking some of the right questions. Well, you two enjoy your lunch. I'll see you next week."

We watched him join his family already seated in a booth across the room. His comments had taken me by surprise; I had thought Jay was up front talking to him about us. Now I didn't know what to believe. Turning to Karen, I asked, "Do you think Jay really wants a relationship with the Lord?"

"I don't know, Julia. I hope so. But it could be an act to get on your good side again. Time will tell if he's for real."

I saw Jay twice the next week, once walking on campus and once in The Coffee Cup. Each time, he acknowledged me with a smile but was careful to keep his distance. I was still struggling with feelings of guilt and had to force myself not to think about the good times we'd had, how exciting it was to be with him those first few weeks of dating.

Meanwhile, life at the sorority house had become a daily trial. I was the accused, presumed guilty before proven innocent. All the girls, including Fran, took turns pleading Jay's case. Even quiet J.R. gave me a hard time. My only way of coping was to count the weeks left to serve out my sentence—only six more to go.

Karen and I were back in church the next Sunday. So was Jay. It was the same scenario: We sat in the front, and he sat in the back. This time, however, I was more relaxed. Pastor Scott's comments in the restaurant had somewhat calmed my fears about Jay's motivation for coming. This week I was able to enjoy the message and even take a few notes.

At the end of the service, Pastor Scott gave an invitation to accept Christ. All heads were bowed, but I could hear people moving to the front of the church for prayer. I raised my eyes for a moment and saw Jay standing up at the altar. Pastor Scott had his hand on Jay's shoulder and was praying for him. I poked Karen next to me and motioned to the front. Seeing Jay, she looked back over at me and smiled. We were both happy for him.

Once everyone had received prayer, several people went down to congratulate those at the altar. Karen and I walked over to where Jay was standing. He seemed glad to see us.

Karen encouraged Jay to start reading his Bible right away. "Try to read a chapter a day," she suggested. "There are some devotional books in the back of the church, too. Pick one up on your way out. There's a page for you to read each day to help you grow as a Christian."

Jay acknowledged Karen's instructions and then looked at me. "Thanks for letting me come here, Julia, especially after what happened between us. Now that I'm really a Christian, I hope we can at least be friends."

"Of course," I answered awkwardly, trying to be nice. While others from the congregation were congratulating him, Karen and I turned and quietly left.

I didn't see Jay again until after dinner on Wednesday. I had decided to study at the library in order to hide from the girls at the sorority house. I was organizing some lecture notes when someone sat down in the chair next to me. I turned to find Jay at my side. He had a new Bible in his hand and a confused look on his face.

"Care to help a fellow Christian out?"

"Sure," I replied, startled by his sudden appearance.

"Karen told me to read the Bible every day, but I don't know what I'm doing. Where should I start?"

"Try the book of John," I suggested. "Then read through the book of Acts and all the epistles."

Jay scanned the table of contents in his Bible. "I found John and Acts, but I don't see anything called Epistle."

I couldn't help but smile when he said that. I had forgotten that all this was new to him. "My fault, Jay. There isn't any book called Epistle. An epistle is just another name for a letter. There are lots of them in the New Testament."

We sat side by side for a while as I showed Jay how the Bible was laid out. He asked questions, and I did my best to answer them. After awhile he suggested we take a break and get a coffee together.

I hesitated for a moment and then agreed, rationalizing that a short walk to the Coffee Cup with Jay would probably be safe. We gathered up our things and exited the building into the night air. It was a refreshing change from the stuffy library.

The service at the café was slow that night, not because it was crowded, but because they were having trouble with the cappuccino machine. Eventually, our orders arrived, and we had a nice talk over our coffees. I had to admit that I was once again enjoying Jay's company. He had a dry sense of humor, and I was reminded of how much I laughed when we were together. The last few weeks had been very lonely for me; it was fun being with him again.

It was already dark by the time we finished our drinks, so Jay offered to escort me back to the sorority house. Again, I figured that just walking home with Jay would be okay. He was a perfect gentleman the whole way, and when we arrived at the front steps, he merely said, "Good night, Julia. Thanks for being my friend."

As I made my way up the stairs, I suddenly realized that I'd been with Jay all night and hadn't felt afraid. Something had definitely changed. Maybe it *would* be possible for us to be friends.

The next time I saw Jay was at church on Sunday. Karen and I had arrived ahead of him. Just as the service was starting, he slipped into our pew and sat down next to me. "Okay if I sit with you guys today?" he whispered.

We both smiled and nodded our approval. Just then, worship began, signaling all three of us to direct our attention toward the front. As Pastor spoke, I noticed that Jay had brought his Bible but was struggling to find the Scripture verses. I knew that with practice, he would find his way around those pages with ease.

After the service, Jay invited both Karen and me out for lunch. We decided on a Chinese restaurant and met him there. He kept us both laughing for the entire meal, and when we were finished eating, he graciously picked up the check.

Karen and I discussed Jay as we drove back to campus. She thought he'd been very charming and that he did seem to have an interest in God now. "Just keep it friends-only, Julia," she warned. "It's still too soon to know if what we're seeing is real."

After church I studied for several hours in my room. Fran was gone with J.R., so I had plenty of peace and quiet. I had finished most of my reading when my cell rang. It was Jay.

"I'm ready for a break. How 'bout you?"

"I was just thinking the same thing," I admitted.

"Text Karen. We can all go see a movie or something."

"Karen's busy finishing a paper for tomorrow."

"Okay, what about you?"

"I guess I can go as long as I'm back by eleven. I have two more chapters to read before class tomorrow."

"No problem. I'll pick you up in fifteen minutes."

The movie was a welcome relief from a long day of studying. Not having eaten since lunch, we stuffed ourselves with popcorn and candy. When the show was over, Jay brought me straight home, keeping his promise to have me back early. It was a little after ten when he walked me to the front stairs of the house. "Do you have time to sit and talk for a minute?" he asked.

Checking my watch, I nodded *yes*. It was such a beautiful spring night that I was glad to have an excuse to stay outside a little longer. There were two concrete benches out on the front lawn. Jay led me over to one, and we sat down.

"We only have four weeks of school left," he began. "Then I'll be graduating, and you'll be packing up to go home. I know you said you didn't want to date me anymore, but things have changed since then. *I've* changed. Why can't we see each other until the end of the semester?"

His question caught me off guard. "I like being with you, Jay, but I don't know if dating again is a good idea. Can we really start over and keep things from getting serious?"

"All I know is that I don't want to spend the next month miserable and alone. It's only for a few weeks. Can't you at least give it a try?"

I looked at his hopeful face and melted. Things *were* different now, and it would be so nice to hang out with him again. After a few moments of hesitation, I reached over and squeezed his hand *okay*.

Jay broke out in his familiar smile and announced, "For that, you get a kiss." He then leaned close to me and softly brushed my lips with his. "Only light kisses allowed," he warned.

Once again, he made me laugh. We talked for a few more minutes before I reminded him about the reading I still had to finish. Reluctantly, Jay walked me back to the stairs and wished me good night.

Recalling Jay's quip about our kissing rule, I was still grinning as I walked through the front door of the sorority house. Suddenly, I noticed Carrie and her roommate sitting on one of the couches in the parlor, giggling. In a sarcastic voice, Carrie called out, "Looks like you decided to give Jay another chance after all." The two of them burst out laughing. They had apparently witnessed our kiss through the window.

I didn't bother to stop and explain. Regardless of what they thought, things were *not* the same between Jay and me. We had a brand new deal going—one they wouldn't understand. I knew that by morning, everyone in the house would have the latest report on us, but I didn't care. Let them think whatever they wanted. It didn't matter. I only had four more weeks to get through.

Chapter 6

Awakened Desire

My goal the next morning was to get ready for class and slip out of the room without waking Fran. Fortunately, I succeeded. I knew she would have the news about Jay and me relayed to her sometime during the day. I'd just have to deal with whatever she had to say when I got back.

When I returned later that afternoon, Fran was leaving to go to a lab. I expected her to be all over me with excitement, listing all the reasons why I'd made the right decision about Jay. She did congratulate me, but didn't seem that surprised. In fact, she looked kind of irritated. Her reaction puzzled me.

As soon as Fran had gone, Theresa came bursting through the door. "Now that you and Jay are back together, are you going to the Spring Fling?"

She was referring to the spring formal annually sponsored by the Greek sororities on campus. It was a ladies' choice dance, one of the main social events of the semester. Posters had been up for weeks, but I hadn't paid any attention to them. Jay and I had broken up, and there wasn't anyone else I wanted to ask.

"I'm not going." I answered, weakly.

"Why not? Everyone in our house will be there. You had a reason when you and Jay were having problems, but now that you guys are back together, you'd be crazy not to go."

"I'd like to, Theresa, but the dance is only two weeks away. I don't have a dress or the extra cash to buy one."

"You can borrow one of mine. I have a closet full of them from high school—take your pick. All you need is a date, so call Jay and ask him. Then come down to my room and you can try on some dresses."

Until that moment, I hadn't considered going to the Spring Fling. Suddenly, I felt an awakened desire to dress up and go to a dance like other girls. For the first time, my parents weren't around to spoil my fun. This was my chance to do something I had always dreamed about, and I was sure that Jay would take me.

He didn't answer his cell when I called, so I just sent him a text message to call me. About an hour later, he did. "Hi, beautiful. Whatever you want, you've got it!"

I laughed and then got right to the point. "I need a date for the Spring Fling. Would you like to take me?"

"Well, only if I get a kiss when I bring you home."

"Oh, I think that can be arranged," I responded coyly.

We talked for several minutes about nothing in particular, kidding back and forth. The minute we hung up, I was out the door and on my way to Theresa's room. By the time I got there, she had several formals already spread out on her bed.

"I assume Jay said *yes*, so try these on," she instructed.

I tried on six of them before making a final decision. We both agreed that the pale pink gown with the spaghetti straps suited me best. Just as I was about to slip out of it and return it to the hanger, Carrie walked in.

"I see someone's going to the dance," she observed.

Theresa was quick to answer for me. "Yeah, she didn't have a dress to wear, but this one's great, isn't it?"

Carrie nodded. "I've got a necklace and earrings that would go perfect with it. Wait here a minute—I'll be right back."

She quickly returned and brought along her roommate, Lindsay, who loaned me a clutch bag. They also got Abby from next door to throw in a pair of her jeweled heels, size seven. Each of the girls gave advice on how I should do my hair and nails. They were having fun making me over, and it was nice being accepted for a change.

Fran was back in our room by the time I returned with my new ensemble. When she saw the dress in my arms, she gave me a hug, so excited I was going to the dance. What a mood swing! Before leaving for her lab, she had seemed on edge. Now she was relaxed and happy. She asked me to try on everything for her and beamed with approval.

"You're not going to believe this, Fran, but at home, I wasn't allowed to go to dances. This will be my first. I hope it's special."

"Oh, it *will* be," Fran said with a knowing smile. I detected a hidden meaning behind her statement, but I had learned not to ask Fran to explain herself. We got along better that way.

That whole week Jay and I found more and more opportunities to be together, studying in the library instead of our rooms and meeting at The Coffee Cup every day after classes. He was reaching out to me as his girlfriend more and more, and I was gradually responding. It was not uncommon to see us holding hands around campus. More times than not, I would feel Jay slip his arm around my shoulder to draw me close as we walked.

Saturday night we decided to go downtown and bowl a couple of games. Afterwards, we walked down to the ice cream shop to get our favorite double dip cones. It was such a perfect night that we ate them as we strolled along the main street. There were quaint little shops nestled between the larger stores and businesses. We had fun window shopping together.

Since we had church in the morning, Jay brought me back to my house by eleven o'clock. As we walked up the front stairs together, he jokingly looked from side to side to make sure that we were alone. "Looks like a safe time to slip in a kiss," he laughed.

Sliding his arms around my waist, he leaned down and kissed me. Then he gave me a hug and said good night. As he made his way to his car, he called out, "I'll pick you up for church at nine-thirty. Then we'll swing by and get Karen."

I was in bed well before midnight, but I was having trouble falling asleep. Something about Jay's kiss kept bothering me. It wasn't the playful, light kiss I had been receiving from him lately, yet there was nothing out of line about it either. Nevertheless, it communicated deep feelings from both of us that were way beyond our agreement to date only until the end of the term. I knew we were probably making a mistake, but I deliberately pushed aside my concerns. The dance was coming up on Friday, and then, in two weeks' time, our relationship would be over.

As I had come to expect, Fran was still sound asleep when I left for church in the morning. Jay was waiting out front right at nine-thirty, and after picking up Karen, we were sitting in our familiar pew at church just in time for the start of the service.

During Pastor Scott's sermon, Jay reached over and took my hand in his. Karen noticed and gave me a look of surprise. Embarrassed, I quickly turned away. For the rest of the service, I concentrated more on avoiding eye contact with Karen than on listening to the message.

After church, Jay offered to buy Karen and me lunch again. We went to a different restaurant this time, an Italian one. I ordered my favorite entrée, but it was hard to enjoy it since I was working so hard to avoid the nonverbal communication I was getting from Karen every time Jay would hold my hand or put his arm around me. I was glad when our meal was finished and we were finally dropping Karen off at her dorm. Before getting out of the car, she looked at me and asked, "Are you going to be in your room later?"

"I should be." I replied.

"Okay. I'll give you a call when I take a study break. Thanks again for lunch, Jay," she added before climbing out of the back seat.

"I know what you want to talk about," I thought with a wince as she shut the car door. Jay dropped me off at my house with a quick kiss goodbye, promising to call me later. He thought we might want to go downtown again for some more ice cream.

When I got back to my room, Fran was gone. I was really appreciating her many absences. It was almost like having my own room. I changed into something comfortable and then began studying at my desk. After a few hours, my cell rang. It was

Karen. "I'm going to take a break soon. How about meeting me at The Coffee Cup in an hour?"

"Sounds good," I lied. "See you there."

I knew Karen wasn't that interested in getting a cappuccino. She wanted to talk to me about Jay. I wasn't in the mood, but I would have to explain about him sooner or later. I figured I might as well get it over with. Besides, Karen had been a good friend to me. I didn't want to brush her off.

A major struggle was going on inside of me. Deep in my heart, I knew it was a mistake to date Jay again. I also knew that Karen was going to confront me about it. Even though she was undoubtedly right, I wasn't ready to give him up just yet. He made me laugh when we were together. Why should I go back to being lonely? I didn't want to think any further ahead than today because today was fun. I convinced myself that tomorrow would work out fine. In a couple of weeks, Jay and I would say our goodbyes. But for now, we could enjoy being together.

I had myself convinced. Now all I had to do was find a way to persuade Karen. I knew her too well to think it was going to be easy. I didn't have time to rehearse a speech either. I needed to get some more reading done before our meeting or I'd be up half the night.

Chapter 7

Warnings

Grabbing my English book, I flopped onto my bed and propped up a pillow behind me. I had only gotten through a few chapters when someone knocked on my door. Calling for the person to come in, I was surprised to see Gretchen walk into my room.

"Can I talk to you for a minute?"

"Sure, have a seat."

Gretchen closed the door and made her way over to the small couch in the corner. Once she sat down, I waited for her to begin.

"I heard you were going to the dance with Jay."

"Theresa talked me into it. She even gave me a dress to wear."

"Look, Julia, I don't think you know what goes on with the guys from the frats here. Have you ever been to Jay's frat house?"

"No, Jay always picks me up downstairs, and we go out somewhere. There's really no reason to go to his frat."

"Good; those guys have their techniques down to a science."

"Techniques?"

"You know, for getting you to sleep with them. Believe me; that's all a lot of them care about. Some guys even use drugs to get what they want. That's how it happened to me."

Gretchen looked away for a brief moment, her eyes moist. She sighed and then forced herself to continue. "I was a virgin when I came to campus, and I had planned to stay that way. I was never really religious, but I did believe in God and had good morals.

"I met Brad in class my first semester, and we started dating. Right away, he pressured me to have sex with him, but I wouldn't. His fraternity brothers were giving him a hard time about not scoring with me. They decided he needed some help.

"The next time I went with Brad to a party at his frat house, his friends put something in my drink. After a while, I started to feel dizzy. Brad said I was probably getting the flu or something and took me up to his room to lie down. When I was too weak to fight him off, he raped me. Then I passed out.

"Hours later, I woke up in bed with Brad and remembered what had happened. When I started to cry hysterically, Brad sat up, put his hand over my mouth, and threatened to hit me if I didn't calm down. He said, 'You girls are so stupid about being a virgin. Well, you're not anymore, so grow up and let's have some fun from now on.' I left early that morning and walked back to my dorm alone. Brad wouldn't even get out of bed to take me home. You know the rest of my story. I told you the night you came into my room."

"Yes, I remember, Gretchen. But how could you keep dating Brad after what he did to you?"

As she answered me, tears slipped down her cheeks. "I felt dirty and worthless after Brad raped me, like no guy would want me after that. Brad wanted to stay with me, so I've stayed with him. He took more than my virginity that night, Julia. He took my self-respect. It's hard to explain, but it's like he owns me now. A few weeks after that night, I pledged and moved into the sorority house."

Gretchen had started to really cry now, so I grabbed some tissues and brought them over to her. Dabbing away her tears, she added, "If you're wondering why Fran's rarely here, it's because she and J.R. are usually up in his room. That means Jay has to find someplace else to go."

I couldn't help but ask, "Is there a reason you're telling me all this?"

"Yes," she admitted. "That night you came into my room, I told you something you could've spread all over campus. But you didn't tell anyone my secret, and I'm really grateful, Julia. I don't know much about Jay, but I do know he's been in that frat for three years. You had trouble with him once; I don't want something even worse to happen to you. I don't want you to feel ashamed for the rest of your life like I do."

"You don't have to feel that way anymore, Gretchen. No matter what you think, God loves you, and He has a lot more for your life. Will you do me a favor?"

"What?"

"I'm meeting a friend at The Coffee Cup in a few minutes. Come with me. You'll like Karen, and I know she'll help you see that you don't have to settle for a guy like Brad."

Gretchen looked a little skeptical, but she agreed to meet me there after first going back to her room to fix her make up. Already a little late, I decided to drive my car down to The Coffee Cup. When I got there, Karen was at our usual table, waiting for me.

Once we ordered, I began telling Karen all about Gretchen and Brad. Karen interrupted me. "If she's going to be here soon, I only have a few minutes to talk to you about Jay. It's obvious you guys are dating again. I thought we agreed it was too soon to tell if Jay was for real."

"We did, but he's been so different lately..."

"I'm still worried, Julia. Even if Jay is a Christian now, he's graduating in a little over two weeks. Where do you see your relationship going long-term?"

"It's not going anywhere long-term. Jay and I agreed to date only until the end of the semester. We're just having fun for a few weeks."

"Jay's crazy about you, Julia; I can't see him walking away from you after graduation. I think you're making a big mistake. I don't want to see you get hurt by him again."

Before I could answer, Gretchen came in and found us at our table. From that point on, I was off the hook, the attention now directed to her. After introductions were made and Gretchen had ordered her food, we spent a few minutes eating and making small talk.

When our conversation finally got around to Brad, Karen told Gretchen about how much Jesus loved her and wanted to be part of her life. Gretchen didn't respond right then with a decision for Christ, but I felt she had received hope that there might be a future for her with God.

As we were leaving, Karen got Gretchen to agree to come to our next Thursday night Bible study, an end-of-the-semester party. Since she had walked down to the restaurant, I invited Gretchen to ride back with me. She wasn't very talkative on the way home. I couldn't tell if she was serious about coming to our next meeting until we got back to the sorority house and she said, "I'm looking forward to going with you Thursday night. Don't forget me."

When I got back to my room, my book was lying on the bed where I had left it. Fran was still out. After my talk with Gretchen, I would have to try hard not to think about where she and J.R. were and what they might be doing.

I grabbed my cell phone that I had accidentally left behind and checked for messages. Jay had left me a text saying he was picking me up at nine o'clock. I had only a few hours to finish reading eight chapters. That meant I would be pulling a late night of studying after Jay brought me home.

Only half of my reading was finished when I received a call from the front desk that Jay was downstairs waiting for me. Slamming my book shut, I picked up my purse and ran down to the parlor. The warnings about Jay from my friends were still on my mind. I wanted to get off campus and think about something else.

The drive downtown was refreshing as Jay and I lowered the windows to let the night air blow in. It was nice being with Jay, laughing and feeling carefree again. Once we reached the ice cream parlor and ordered our cones, I felt even better. I had eaten a snack with the girls earlier, but it was nine-thirty by now, and I was hungry.

It was a beautiful spring evening, so we walked for a while down the main street. Jay spotted an empty bench in front of one of the little shops, and we sat down to finish our cones. We stayed there for over an hour talking and laughing, but all too soon, it was time to leave and return to the books. When we got back to my house, Jay was in a playful mood. Taking me in his arms, he danced me up the steps.

"Need to practice for Friday night," he explained. "I'll have the prettiest girl at the dance." Smiling, he pulled me close and whispered, "I'm never happier than when I'm with you, Julia." His kiss was deep and lingering, but he never lost control. "I'll call you tomorrow," he promised as he walked away.

I stayed up until two a.m., reading and preparing for my early class. After I had climbed into bed and turned out the light, Fran came in. She was undressed and in bed herself in a matter of minutes, unaware that I was still awake. She must have been tired because I could tell by her breathing that she had fallen asleep right away.

My body was exhausted, too, but my mind couldn't rest. It kept replaying my conversation with Gretchen about the fraternity guys. Had Jay been a part of that wild frat life before he met me? I didn't know. True, he had lost control with me in the past, but I believed that Jay had experienced a change in his life, and I felt safe with him now.

Karen's words kept repeating in my mind as well. She had warned me that Jay was in too deep to want to turn back. She just had to be wrong. Jay and I had promised to say goodbye after his graduation. Everything would work out the way we'd planned. I was sure of it.

The whole time I was in bed thinking, I could see the outline of Theresa's pink satin formal hanging on the outside of my closet door. Smiling, I pictured myself gliding across the dance floor with Jay. "It'll be a special night for both of us," I reassured myself as I finally drifted off to sleep.

Chapter 8

Living the Lie

Not getting much sleep the night before, I had to drag myself out of bed for my early morning class. I nodded off twice during the lecture, but the discussion period at the end helped to revive me. Since my schedule was free until mid-afternoon, I decided to go back to the house and sleep for a while.

When I got back to our room, I remembered that Fran was still in class. Now I could rest without being disturbed. My head barely hit the pillow before I was fast asleep. A couple hours later, I heard my cell ringing. Barely able to open my eyes, I fumbled around and snatched it off my nightstand. It was Jay calling to set up a time to meet me. We decided to grab a quick sandwich together at five and then spend some time studying at the library.

Checking the clock, I saw that my afternoon class was starting in ten minutes. I was glad that Jay had called when he did! I had almost slept through that class. Quickly freshening up, I grabbed my book bag and made a swift exit to avoid being late. Running most of the way, I made it just in time.

After class, I pulled out my cell to text my mom because of an email I'd gotten from her a few days ago. It had been perfectly normal except for the very end, which read: "The Holy Spirit has me interceding for you in prayer an hour every day, Julia. I don't understand why, do you? I'm still waiting for you to open up and tell me. Love, Mom."

Before answering back, I stopped by my old dorm to visit Toni to find out if she had said anything to alarm my parents when they last phoned. She wasn't aware of anything. Fortunately, my mom called while I was there. She seemed relieved to finally catch me in what she thought was my room. We had a nice mother-daughter conversation, during which I assured her that everything was fine. I felt confident after her call that my mom's mind was more at ease, but I still wanted to send her a quick text today to avoid any further suspicion.

I wasn't proud of the way I was deceiving my mom and dad. Living the lie was hard, but I thought it was better than hurting my parents with the truth. In a little over two weeks, I would be back home, and this whole mess would be over.

I finished my text, hit *send*, and then hurried to meet Jay. We both arrived at the campus café a little after five. By then I was so hungry I was shaking. Except for a few crackers I'd eaten on the way to my morning class, I hadn't had anything in my stomach all day.

Jay was in a talkative mood, which suited me fine. It allowed me to inhale my hamburger and fries without much interruption. He was all excited about the post-graduation job he had accepted. The company had given him an excellent starting salary, great benefits, and even initial housing for him in one of their condominiums.

"My District Manager called and asked me to drive down and meet him this week," Jay announced. "He's going to be out of town my first few days on the job, so he wants to show me my office and condo this Thursday. I'll leave early in the morning and won't get back until late. But don't worry your pretty head," he reassured me. "I haven't forgotten our big date on Friday."

I was glad to hear that Jay's plans were working out so well. It would make it easier when we parted, knowing that he had a new and exciting place to go next. He would be so involved in his new job that he would soon forget about me.

Once we were done eating, neither of us felt like spending the night studying. The closer we came to the end of the semester, the harder it was to apply ourselves. The weather was inviting us to come out and play, but the pressure of keeping up our grades won out. We compromised by going to the library for an hour or two.

The time passed quickly, and before we knew it, we were finished for the night. As we left the building, it was starting to sprinkle. We were on foot and without an umbrella, but since it was such a warm evening, we took our time walking back.

Gradually, the mild sprinkling turned into a heavy shower. We ran the rest of the way to the front steps of my sorority house. By that time, the rain had subsided and we were both completely soaked. We laughed about how funny each of us looked with wet, dripping hair.

Jay drew me close and explained that he had a big project he needed to work on during the next couple of days, that he might be hard to reach. "If I don't answer my phone, just leave a message; I'll get back to you as soon as I can. I'll tell you all about it Friday night," he vowed mysteriously.

"Why can't you tell me now?"

He lightly touched his forehead to mine. "Girls who ask too many questions spoil big surprises."

Before I could think of a witty answer, he planted a big kiss on my lips. But it wasn't like the lingering kiss I'd received the night before. This time our faces were both so wet from the rain, his lips slid right off mine and onto my cheek.

Surprised, we laughed until our sides ached. Then Jay noticed that I was starting to shiver. He gave me a quick hug and said good night so I could get inside and out of my wet clothes.

We didn't get to see each other over the next few days. Jay had two class projects due that Friday, and since he'd be gone all day Thursday, he would naturally have to work ahead to have them finished before he left on his trip. Yet neither of those projects could have been the one he alluded to in the rain Monday night. Jay had something else up his sleeve, something that apparently had to do with me. I wouldn't see him again until the dance on Friday, so I would simply have to wait to find out.

Thursday was always a light class day for me, giving me time to run errands and catch up on personal things. That Thursday I went downtown to buy ingredients for the cookies I was making for my Bible study group. My plan was to bake them early in the day while getting some laundry done at the same time.

When I returned from the store, Gretchen was just coming down from her room. We stopped to talk in the lobby. I was glad to hear she was still planning on going with me to the meeting. When she found out that I had to make cookies, she offered to help me. Our sorority house had a kitchen we could use. After I threw in my first load of clothes, we started baking.

"How does Brad feel about you going with me tonight?" I finally asked as I pulled a cookie sheet from the oven.

Her answer was sad. "I'd be afraid to tell Brad I was going to a Bible study. But he'll never know. On Thursdays he plays poker with some guys from his fraternity. It's the one night I'm free to do what I want."

I didn't know what to say, so I changed the subject. Once the cookies were all baked and cooled enough to wrap, we both went to our rooms to study for a while.

I did some more laundry and read for a couple of hours before finally setting my alarm and taking a nap. When the buzzer went off, it awakened me from such a deep sleep that I was tempted to turn it off and return to my pillow. But remembering Gretchen and how much she was looking forward to the party, I managed to get enough adrenaline going to get up and start getting ready.

Yawning, I rummaged through my closet looking for something to wear. After much deliberation, I decided on a simple blue blouse with a pair of jeans. My hair wasn't cooperating with me, so I finally threw it up in a ponytail. After putting on a little lip gloss, I was set to go. Balancing the platter of cookies in one hand, I scooped up my keys off the dresser, slid my purse up over my shoulder, and headed for the door. When I opened it, Gretchen was standing on the other side.

"I'm ready!" she cheerfully announced.

"Okay, let's take my car."

We exchanged the usual girl talk on the drive over. As we did, I caught a glimpse of a different girl from the one I had gotten to know at the sorority house. In my first few weeks there, Gretchen had appeared to be confident and happy, like she had it all together. My private conversations with her, however, revealed a young woman who was guilt-ridden, miserable, and very insecure.

But there in the car, away from Brad and the influence of the house, she seemed wide-eyed and innocent and very much at ease. I wondered if I was seeing the real Gretchen for the first time. Perhaps this was the girl she had been before Brad came along, the one that God wanted to rescue and lead into a new and better life.

When we arrived at our destination, it took several minutes to find a parking space. It was Gretchen's eagle eye that eventually saw an open spot just down the street. We quickly pulled into it, jumped out of the car, and started toward the building, cookies in hand.

Chapter 9

Seeing the Truth

After a long walk and a steep climb up the stairs of the building, we finally arrived at the party. Karen was waiting at the door to greet us. After passing off the cookies, we took Gretchen around together and introduced her to everyone.

The leader of our study group was a junior named Gary, a linebacker on the football team. He stood well over six feet and weighed about 230 pounds. Needless to say, people paid attention when he was around. Once I slapped him on the arm trying to make a point; it felt like hitting concrete.

Gary started the meeting with prayer, and then we broke up in groups of six to play Charades. Karen and Gary called over for Gretchen and me to be on their team. Chad and Kenny, two of Gary's teammates, joined us to round out our number to six.

As might be expected, we played the girls against the guys. Feeling dwarfed next to these big football players, we girls teased that this was a contest of brains against brawn. The guys pretended to be offended, and we all tried to win for the next hour.

As we played, everyone in our circle seemed to be having fun. I was proud of the way my Christian friends were making Gretchen feel at home. Glancing around the room, I saw that the other teams were having a great time, too.

In a strange way, I felt like a newcomer myself. These people had been a regular part of my life since starting college, yet somehow I had failed to appreciate them. They were obviously a lot of fun and loved and supported each other. So why hadn't I noticed before just how great they were? I knew the answer in my heart: I had joined this group looking for a boyfriend, not for Christian friends.

Disappointed in myself for being so shallow, I didn't feel like playing anymore. But I got back into the game, not wanting to spoil Gretchen's fun. I was glad when Gary finally looked at his watch and announced that it was time to quit and head for the food table. Chad was asked to pray over the refreshments, and when he finished, we lined up to fill our plates. Gary put on some music while everyone found a chair or place on the floor to sit and eat.

As I sat sampling the food, I had a flashback to the wild frat party I'd gone to months before. I silently compared it to the party I was at now. At both places, you could hear music and laughter coming from all directions of the room as everybody had fun with friends. But the feel of this party was totally different.

The people at the two parties were different, too. Most of the ones at the frat house were looking for happiness, but using each other to get it. Most of the people at this party had already experienced happiness in their relationship with Jesus, and they were helping others to find it. As I reviewed that last thought in my mind, I realized I had gotten lost somewhere between those two worlds over the past couple of months.

Now I felt uneasy about going to the Spring Fling, but I didn't see any way I could back out at the last minute. Jay was excited about taking me, and the girls at the house had been so nice about loaning me their things. The dance was less than twenty-four hours away; I would have to go.

Hearing Gretchen laughing in the distance brought my attention back to the party again. I noticed that my guest had finished eating already and was talking to Gary. Tossing my plate in the trash, I slowly made my way over to where they were standing.

Gary smiled as I joined them and said, "I just found out that Gretchen was a cheerleader for one of my high school's biggest rivals. I can't believe she used to cheer against me."

"Whatever," Gretchen laughed. "The guys on our team used to call Gary *The Wall*. They said running into him was like hitting a ton of bricks."

Gary grinned and admitted, "Some other schools picked up on that name. It stuck with me all through high school."

Gretchen went on. "You know, I met you once at the movies. I was standing in line with a big tub of popcorn, waiting to get into the show. You bumped into me, making me spill half of it. You were totally nice and bought me another tub. I felt honored to get so much attention from the famous *Wall*."

Gary gave us a puzzled look and just shrugged his shoulders. Gretchen smiled at him. "I figured you didn't remember me."

"Sorry, Gretchen. When I was in high school, I was more into weights and football than girls. But I wouldn't forget you if the same thing happened now."

"Too late," I kidded. "She already has a boyfriend."

"Really, why didn't you guys come together?" Gary asked.

Neither of us expected Gretchen's reaction. With tears in her eyes, she blurted out, "He would never come here. He doesn't even know I came tonight, and I don't know what he'd do if he found out."

"What kind of guy is this?" Gary responded, checking out her left hand. "I don't see a ring, so you're not engaged. Even if you were, he doesn't own you."

"That's where you're wrong," Gretchen said quietly, looking down.

Gary answered gently, "He does *not* own you, Gretchen. But it looks like he's convinced you he does. It's time you start seeing the truth."

Several of the people around us could tell that Gary was ministering to Gretchen. Not wanting to interrupt, they left us alone and went on with their own conversations.

"So," Gary continued, "does this guy go to school here?"

"Yes," Gretchen replied, wiping away tears with her hand. "He's a senior in one of the fraternities."

Just then, Karen walked up to give Gretchen some tissues. Gary asked her to stay with us. Looking around, he spotted a more private place in the corner of the room where we could all sit down and talk.

Once we were seated, Gary resumed the conversation. "I know all about the frats at Tyler. I came here to play football, and when I got on campus, they were all after me to join. I didn't know much about being in a fraternity, only that it was a status symbol and a lot more fun than dorm life. Anyway, I decided to join one my second semester.

"I soon found out that guys in the frat respected you for scoring with girls. So, to fit in, I started to party and sleep with lots of girls. I never had to use force or drugs to get what I wanted.

Most of them were more than willing, and the ones that weren't, I pressured until they gave in.

"I learned that lots of girls cave in to guilt and fear. First, you try guilt. You say you're in love with them and that if they really loved you, they'd do what you want. With others, fear works better. You threaten to stop dating them if they won't sleep with you. The insecure ones will give in because they think it's better than being alone. Some of the girls were virgins, and we guys considered them the ultimate score. We continually bragged to each other about our sex lives.

"During the first semester of my sophomore year, I met a guy in my science class named Jim. We worked a lot of lab time together, and he really helped me out. He invited me to come to this study group, but I wasn't interested in God or church or anything that even sounded religious. Jim never gave up, though. He still invited me every week. I was grateful for the time he spent tutoring me, so I finally agreed to go.

"It only took one meeting to get through to me, Gretchen. When I heard what Jim read from the Bible and saw people praying like they knew Jesus as a real person, I broke down and *cried*. Embarrassing, but true. Deep down in my heart, I didn't feel good about what was going on in my life. I wasn't involved much with girls before I came to college, but after joining the fraternity, I'd become a complete jerk, sleeping with anyone that came along. No matter how much I was told it was the cool thing to do, it just wasn't me. Jim explained the plan of salvation to me, and I asked Christ to be my Savior and Lord that night.

"Jim had his own apartment off campus. He encouraged me to move out of the frat house and stay with him. He said I couldn't live in that environment and grow in my relationship with God. I had come to trust and respect Jim, so I took his advice and moved out the next day. When the guys found out why I was leaving, I got ridiculed big time. I didn't care. There had been such a change on the inside of me that I was even surprising myself.

"Over the next few months, Jim taught me how to study my Bible and pray. When I saw just how wrong my lifestyle had been, I started having major problems with guilt. What haunted me most was how I had used the girls I dated. Jim worked and prayed with me until I was able to receive God's forgiveness for what I'd done. It took me even longer to forgive myself.

"Jim sat me down one night, just like I'm doing with you, Gretchen. He said, 'You can't change the wrong choices you made yesterday. But you can make better choices today and then help others to do the same thing.' Once I started making the right choices, it got easier and easier. Eventually, Jim helped me turn my guilt into a passion to help other people avoid the mistakes I'd made.

"I couldn't undo the damage I had done to the girls I'd used, but I could ask for their forgiveness, and I did. I also shared with them the change that Christ had made in my life, giving them an opportunity to let God repair and replace what I couldn't. Now I try to warn girls about what goes on here and tell them how to protect themselves. These things happen all over campus, not just at the frats.

"When Jim graduated last year, he turned the leadership of this group over to me. I have Karen and Tina work with the girls that come to our group. This isn't a singles' club or a dating service. We're interested in building Christ into your life, not romance.

"I work with the guys on campus, trying to show them that being a man has to do with their *character*, instead of their sex life. Chad and Kenny were both living pretty crazy when I met them. Now they're great men of God and work with me, too."

Gretchen was quietly taking in Gary's every word.

"I've only known you a few hours, Gretchen," Gary continued, "and already I see how special you are. I don't know what this jerk has done to you, but I can guess. That kind of guy won't stick with a girl for long unless he's getting her to do what he wants.

"No matter what's happened with your boyfriend, you can't change it. But you can change what you're doing now. With God's help, you can choose to walk away and start again. You don't have to stay with him. The only hold he has on you is in your own mind. But if you do decide to stay with him, you'll live out all the bad consequences that go with that choice.

"Before you came tonight, Karen told me that she explained to you how to give your life to Christ. So, now you have to make another choice: to accept God's offer or reject it. I don't expect you to make a decision tonight. I just want you to know that if you want to get out of your relationship with this guy, we'll be here for you. What's his name anyway?"

"Brad."

"Okay, obviously you're afraid of this Brad. Well, I'm not. I want you to take the next couple of days and think about what you want to do—not what you think you *have* to do. If you decide to break it off with him and he gives you a rough time, call me. I'll be there to help you. I'm going to give you my number. I always keep my cell with me. If I can't come for some reason, I'll send either Chad or Kenny." Gary paused for a moment to gauge Gretchen's reaction. "Will you at least promise me you'll think about what I just said?"

Gretchen smiled gratefully at him and assured him she would. Gary was already writing down his number when he responded, "Good choice, Gretchen. That's how winners start out, making one good choice at a time. You'd better go ahead and memorize this number. In an emergency, you might not have time to find this piece of paper."

I looked around and noticed that people were starting to leave. The four of us prayed with Gretchen for a few minutes before we left the building together. We walked Karen to her car first. Then Gary walked Gretchen and me to my car. As we were getting in, he said, "You've still got two weeks to work on her, Julia. Just think of yourself as her Jim." With that, Gary turned and headed for his truck.

Gretchen was very quiet on the ride home. She was apparently keeping her promise to Gary to think about what he'd said. Tonight was probably the first time in a long time that she envisioned her future without Brad.

It was almost eleven o'clock when we got back to the house. Reaching our floor, I said good night as Gretchen turned to unlock the door to her room. Calling for me to wait a minute, she asked me a question that caught me off guard. "Julia, you believe the way Gary and the others in the group do. So, what made you decide to join this sorority?"

"Good question," I thought. Feeling a little embarrassed, I walked back down the hallway to her door and tried to explain. "Well, I was raised all my life in a Christian home, and there were certain things my parents wouldn't let me do. So, when I came to college, I wanted to experience all the fun I thought I'd missed in high school. For once, my parents weren't around to stop me. But after moving in here, I can see that some kinds of fun have really high price tags. I've decided that I don't want to pay those prices, and it's time for me to get back to where I belong.

"I haven't mentioned it, but next semester I'm out of here and back to the dorm. I'm looking for a roommate, by the way. Let me know if anyone comes to mind," I said with a *think-about-it* smile to Gretchen. Then I gave her a hug and told her to come down and see me anytime she wanted to talk.

When I opened the door to my room, Fran was already in bed. Not wanting to awaken her and chance a late-night discussion about anything, I undressed in the dark. Completely drained, I was more than ready to crash for the night. The dance was the following evening, but I wasn't as excited about going anymore. My mind was on Gretchen and all that had happened at the meeting.

Quietly, I slid between my sheets and settled into a comfortable position. Just before falling asleep, my heart cried out for Gretchen in prayer: *"Lord, please help her to see that she can walk away from the past and into a new life with You, just as Gary did."*

Chapter 10

A Night of Regrets

I awoke the next morning at nine. As I sat up and stretched, I glanced at my closet door and saw the formal I'd be wearing that night. Throughout high school, I had dreamed of dressing up and going to a dance. Now that my dream was coming true, I made up my mind to enjoy it.

The ring of my cell phone startled me, interrupting my thoughts. It was Jay. "Good morning, sleepyhead. I got back too late last night to call you. Excited about our big date?"

"If it means being with you," I replied playfully. "What time are you picking me up?"

"The dance starts at eight, so be ready by seven-thirty. That'll give us some time to take pictures before we leave."

"Perfect."

After we hung up, I had to hurry and get ready for a lecture at ten o'clock. Right before I walked out the door, Fran came out of the shower. "Hey, Julia. Ready for your first dance?"

"Definitely! I think we'll all have a great time."

Shrugging, Fran murmured, "Some of us more than others."

Fran had a talent for making statements only she understood, but being pressed for time, I didn't ask for an explanation. I just mumbled some parting words of my own and left.

I had three classes on Fridays. Once they were over, I drove downtown to buy some makeup and nylons. When I finished shopping, I bought a sandwich and drink from one of the outside vendors and found a picnic table nearby. It was a bright, sunshiny day; it felt good to eat outdoors. On my drive in, I'd caught the weather forecast on the radio. Thankfully, it was supposed to be warm all evening, perfect since I didn't have a wrap to wear over my dress.

By four-thirty I was back in my room, painting my nails for the dance. Although I had a lot of studying to do over the weekend, the rest of the day was dedicated to getting ready for my big night. Once my nails were done, I decided to take a short nap while they finished drying. To be safe, I set my alarm so I wouldn't oversleep.

Fran roused me slightly when she came in a little before six and headed for the shower. She was just coming out when my alarm went off. "My turn," I announced.

Theresa had volunteered to fix girls' hair for the dance. A few of us took her up on her offer. I wanted to wear mine up, so I needed to have it dried and ready for her when she came in.

From six o'clock on, the atmosphere in the whole house changed. Girls busily went in and out of showers, hair dryers turned on and off down the halls, and the fragrances of different perfumes floated from room to room. The noise level increased as girls shouted back and forth to each other asking for opinions on jewelry and shoes.

I had just finished drying my hair when Theresa peeked in the doorway to see if I was ready. I nodded that I was, and she tackled the job with confidence. It only took twenty minutes, but when she was done, I looked like I'd gone to a professional.

Theresa wore her hair short and had already finished hers before working on me. "One more and I can get dressed," she said. "Carrie wants a French twist; that shouldn't take too long."

"Thanks, Theresa," I shouted after her as she rushed out the door.

I was putting on my makeup when Fran called to me from the other side of the room. She asked me to look in her top drawer for a hair clip she had forgotten to pull out. Her nails were drying, and she didn't want to mess up her manicure. Although she was shooting one description after another, I was having trouble finding the exact one.

Noticing a rectangular box in the front section of the drawer, I picked it up to check inside. Just as I was removing the lid, my eye spied Fran's clip wedged in the upper corner of the drawer. Returning my attention to the box, I saw what looked like an opened pregnancy test inside. Quickly replacing the cover, I put the box back in its place, grabbed the clip, and told Fran that I'd found it.

As I finished putting on my makeup, I thought about the pregnancy test in Fran's drawer. Maybe the results had something to do with her comment about some having more fun than others that night. If the test was positive, was she planning to tell J.R. at the dance? I knew that their sleeping together wasn't right, but I couldn't help hoping, for Fran's sake, that the test was negative.

My makeup done, I slipped into Theresa's formal and put on the necklace and earrings I had borrowed from Carrie. Stepping into Abby's shoes, I picked up Lindsay's handbag and paused for one final gaze in the mirror. I had to admit I was happy with the way I looked. Everything fit perfectly, my hair looked great, and my nails were flawless.

So why did I feel so disappointed? Suddenly, I realized that I'd always pictured my parents fussing over me the night of my first dance, taking lots of pictures, waving at the door as my date and I drove off. It made me sad that my parents weren't part of this special night. In fact, they didn't even know about it.

As I studied my reflection, I saw that nothing I was wearing was mine—and neither was the life I'd been living for the past semester. The young woman I saw in the mirror was like a stranger to me. I was anxious to go home and be Julia again.

When I got down to the parlor, there were several guys waiting for their dates. Jay was one of them. It was the first time I'd seen him in a suit; he looked exceptionally handsome. When he saw me, his face lit up. Walking over, he gave me a kiss. "You look absolutely beautiful, Julia. This is a night we'll remember for a long time."

Since Fran hadn't come down yet, J.R. offered to take some pictures of us. As he said *smile* before each shot, I couldn't help but wonder how much he'd be smiling if he knew about the test in his girlfriend's drawer. Just then, Fran walked into the parlor, and Jay volunteered to be their photographer.

A few minutes later, we were on our way to the dance. As Jay drove, he quickly recapped all that had happened on his trip. He said that he really liked his District Manager and the office where he'd be working. Then he showed me some pictures of his new condominium. It was really nice, fully furnished and only a short distance from the pool and weight room at the clubhouse.

Listening to Jay share his plans made me feel even more confident that he'd keep our agreement to part as friends in two weeks. We could be grateful for the time we'd spent together, be mature enough to say goodbye, and then move on with our lives.

When we finally arrived at the dance, Jay stopped me outside the entrance and hugged me. "I really missed you yesterday, Julia. You owe me the goodnight kiss I missed out on last night."

I happily gave it to him and we went inside. The band was already playing with couples dancing in the center of the dimly lit room. The tables looked beautiful with linen cloths, glimmering candles, and fresh flowers. Jay found a place for us at one of the round tables close to the dance floor. As soon as I set my purse down, he took my hand and led me out on the floor.

"Tonight's your night," he whispered in my ear. "We're going to dance it away."

Sheepishly, I admitted, "I'm not a very good dancer, Jay."

"Well, I am," he boasted. "Just follow me. You'll be fine."

As the evening wore on, I realized that Jay had meant what he said about dancing the night away! Other than sitting for the dinner that was served, we were on the dance floor the whole time. Jay was an excellent dancer and had fun teaching me the latest steps. Some of them he seemed to be making up as we went along.

I caught myself continually watching for Fran and J.R., trying to figure out what was going on between them. It was so crowded, I had trouble keeping track of them. I finally gave up.

I also saw Gretchen and Brad off and on as they were dancing. I was hoping she was ready to dump him. They were sitting at a table across the room, so it was hard to tell how they were getting along.

Theresa had headed up the dance committee and was doing her usual fine job of playing the social butterfly. It was obvious that she really loved people, and I'd come to appreciate her over the past semester.

Sitting at our table, I noticed that some of the couples around us were spiking their punch. Other than that, the evening was pretty calm. Before the final song began, Jay signaled to me that it was time to leave. We'd been dancing almost continuously, and I was more than ready to go. The shoes I had borrowed from Abby were killing my feet by then. I couldn't wait to slip them off once we got to the car.

Grabbing my purse off the table, we said goodbye to some friends and left. What a relief to walk out of the noisy reception hall and into the peaceful quiet of night.

I had no idea where Jay was taking me after the dance. I didn't ask. He had already warned me that *girls who ask too many questions spoil big surprises.* It was obvious that he had something else planned by the way he was smiling as we drove through town and then down by the lake. Countless stars filled the sky, and the moon was out, shining on the water. Just as the weatherman had predicted, it was a beautiful evening.

As we passed by the park, I noticed a charming white gazebo on the lawn down near the water.

Much to my surprise, Jay suddenly stopped the car. "Okay, we're here. Time for the rest of your special night."

With that, he jumped out of the car, ran around to open my door, and gently helped me out. Grinning, he went to his trunk and removed a small round table and two padded folding chairs. He also unloaded a backpack. After slinging it over his shoulder, he asked me to wait by the car until he came back for me. Then he walked down the hill to the gazebo below. I was amazed that he could carry all of that in one trip, but he made it down there without dropping a thing.

Although he was some distance away, I could see him busily setting up the table in the gazebo. After covering it with a white tablecloth and arranging some things from his backpack on top, he carefully positioned the chairs. I couldn't make out exactly what he was doing, but I was fascinated by how efficiently he was doing it. When he was done, he walked back toward me with his hand extended. "Everything's ready. The only thing I need now is the girl of my dreams."

We both laughed and started toward the gazebo hand in hand. As I came closer, I could see that Jay had set out fruit, cheese and crackers, a bottle of sparkling grape juice, and two champagne glasses. "What's the occasion?" I inquired, holding his hand as we climbed the steps.

"I told you this was your night, Julia. Actually, it's our night. I wanted it to be special, one we would always remember."

Guiding me over to the table, he seated me and then poured the grape juice into the glasses. Moving his chair next to mine, he sat down and raised his glass to make a toast. "Here's to us and to tonight."

I lifted my glass and lightly touched his, making the familiar clink before we each took a sip. Then Jay set his glass down, leaned over, and sweetly kissed me. Taking my hand, he said, "I haven't told you much about my parents, Julia. In fact, there are a few things about my life that I want to share with you.

"My parents are important people where I come from, Julia. Both of them are workaholics, and I rarely see either of them. Growing up, they were constantly traveling or working late, so I was basically raised by the nannies they hired for me.

"My parents gave me everything most people want: a huge home, designer clothes, brand new cars, spending money, and even an education at the college of my choice. They gave me everything except what I wanted and needed—their attention.

"When I came here to Tyler, I was looking for more than an education; I was looking for love. My sophomore year I got caught up in fraternity life and all that went with it. But by the time I got to this last year, I was feeling emptier and more alone than I had when I first came to school. Even though I was sick of the whole frat scene, I only had one more semester to stick it out.

"Then one night I saw you at a party. From that moment, my life began to change. It wasn't just that you were beautiful, Julia. I've been with lots of pretty girls. There was something else about you that drew me in a way I can't explain. All I knew for sure was that I had to get to know you.

"When J.R. told me he knew you, I couldn't believe my luck. I figured getting a date with you would be easy. As you know, it wasn't. For almost a month, getting you to go out with me was all I could think about. Finally, I got the chance to talk to you at The Coffee Cup, and you agreed to go out with me.

"I'm not sure how long we'd been dating when I realized that I'd fallen in love with you. You were different from any girl I'd ever met, and you made me feel loved for the first time in my life. But then I got carried away that night in the car and almost lost you. I don't want that to happen again.

"I know we promised we'd only see each other until school was out, but I have a better plan. You know that I have a good job after graduation. But I never told you that my grandfather died a year ago, leaving me a trust fund with a monthly income as well.

"I checked things out Thursday when I went down to meet my District Manger. There's a college just fifteen minutes from my condo where you could finish getting your degree. I have more than enough money to take care of us, Julia, if you'll just say the word. I want to take you with me when I leave after graduation. I love you, Julia, and I'm asking you to marry me."

Before I could say a word, he reached into his pocket, pulled out a ring, and slipped it onto my finger. "Here's a little inducement," he added with a smile.

I was in shock. I had on my finger one of the most incredible engagement rings I'd ever seen. The diamond must have been at least a carat and was set with three large baguettes on either side. It was breathtaking, to say the least. Instantly, I recalled Karen's words that day in The Coffee Cup: "I can't see him walking away from you after graduation."

I sat there, speechless, not knowing what to say. How could I tell him what I was feeling? He was the one to break the silence.

"I can tell you're overwhelmed, Julia. I am, too—with love for you." Then he stood me up, gathered me in his arms, and kissed me.

I couldn't believe what was happening. Now what was I going to do? Instinctively, I pushed away from him and stepped back. My reaction surprised him, and he looked at me for an explanation. Taking his hand, I tried to find the right words.

"Jay, I *do* care for you, but I can't marry you. I'm not ready to marry anyone. When we were together, marriage was the furthest thing from my mind. I honestly thought we could date until school was over, but now I see that was a big mistake. I haven't been honest about my life for months, Jay. My parents don't have a clue that I'm living in a sorority house, and they know nothing about you. I need to go home and see if I can find myself again."

Hurt, Jay released his hold on my hand, letting it drop. Moving away from me, he walked to the other side of the gazebo and leaned against the railing. He remained quiet for a while with his back toward me, apparently fighting back tears. Without turning around, he finally spoke. "I got a call from my parents this morning saying they're still overseas on business and won't make it back in time for my graduation. I guess I'm right back to where I was before meeting you—all alone."

Now I was fighting back tears. Jay was not only dealing with my refusal, but also with his parents' total disregard for his feelings. Even though I couldn't do anything about his problem with his parents, I needed to take responsibility for the pain I was causing him. There was really nothing to say except, "I'm so sorry, Jay. I never wanted to hurt you."

Crossing the wooden floor, I removed the engagement ring from my hand and slid it back into his suit pocket. Jay didn't move. For the longest time, he just stood there, staring out at the lake. Finally, he turned away and started gathering his things together. I watched in awkward silence and then helped him carry everything back to his car and place it in the trunk again. Neither of us said anything on the drive home.

When Jay pulled up in front of the house to let me out, he reached over and took my hand. "Julia, I sprung this idea on you without any warning, but I know we love each other. Please take a few days to think about it before you make a decision."

I nodded that I would. As I turned to open the car door, he handed me the pictures of his condominium. "Look at these again and try to see yourself living there with me."

I knew they wouldn't change my mind, but I took them anyway. Jay pulled me back to kiss me one last time, and we both said good night as I got out of the car.

When I got back to my room, I was alone. Carefully, I returned Theresa's formal to its hanger and placed all the accessories I had borrowed on my dresser. It felt good to finally crawl into bed after my nightly ritual of removing my makeup and brushing my teeth.

Once my alarm was set, I turned out the light and pulled up the covers. Lying there in the dark, I began to relive the last few hours. Like Cinderella, I'd gone to the ball, danced with Prince Charming, and made him fall in love with me. Only in my story, I came home knowing I had broken the prince's heart. Sadly, my fairy-tale evening had turned out to be a night of regrets.

As I reflected on how much I had hurt Jay, I saw something for the first time. In all my girl-hood fantasies, I was always the center of attention, the fair princess that was being pursued, admired, and rescued. Oddly enough, I had never bothered to think about the prince and all the sacrifices he was making for me. Not once did I see myself doing anything for him.

The conclusion was obvious: the princess was an immature and selfish young woman. I was glad Fran hadn't come in yet. I was an emotional wreck, and once more, I cried myself to sleep.

Chapter 11

Making Choices

When I woke up the next morning, I looked over at Fran's bed to find her jeans and T-shirt still tossed across her pillow, just as they had been before we left for the dance. That meant she hadn't come home. She'd been late getting in before, but this was the first time she had stayed out all night. Suspecting what I did about Fran and J.R., I couldn't help but worry. Quickly, I threw on some sweats to run down the hall and see if Carrie knew anything. As I rushed out the door, I practically collided with Gretchen in the hallway.

Startled, she laughed and said, "I need to talk to you, Julia. I've been up for over an hour, but I wasn't sure if you were awake yet. I was about to tap on your door when you almost ran me over. Are you going somewhere?"

"Just down the hall. But I can go in a minute. Come on in."

As soon as we were in my room, Gretchen told me that she had broken up with Brad after the dance. With schoolgirl-like excitement, she began her story:

I'd been thinking about my relationship with Brad since that night talking with
you guys. Gary was right. The only hold
Brad had on me was in my own mind, and
I was tired of letting him ruin my life. I finally realized that being alone was better
than being with the wrong guy.

Anyway, I wanted to break up with
him, but I was afraid of what Brad might
do. I figured it would be safest to do it
somewhere in public, but it was too loud at
the dance. Besides, we couldn't really talk
in front of everyone.

Neither of us had eaten much at the
dance, so Brad wanted to get something on
the way home. We found a diner that was
still open and sat in a booth by the window.
When our food came, I simply told him
that I was tired of being used by him sexually and in every other way, that he'd have
to find himself another girl because we
were finished. Furious, he reached over
and clutched my wrist so tightly that it
brought tears to my eyes. Then he said we
weren't finished until *he* said so and that
he'd prove it to me when we got back to
the car.

I knew Brad wasn't joking, so while
we were eating, I went to the restroom.
When I got inside, I pulled out my cell
phone and called Gary. He didn't answer,

so I sent him a text message telling him where I was and that I needed help. I waited for a while, turned off my phone, and went back to the table with Brad.

He was almost finished eating by then, but I still had a full plate. I ate slowly, hoping that Gary would get my message and show up before Brad was ready to go. I tried to kill more time by ordering dessert, but Brad wasn't in the mood to pamper me. He called the server over and paid the check.

I had to find another way to stall, so while I was sliding out of my seat, I opened my purse and spilled everything out on the floor under our booth. Irritated, Brad swore at me and crawled underneath the table to pick everything up.

Suddenly, I heard Gary say, "Need some help there?" Reaching down, he grabbed Brad by his arm and literally lifted him to his feet. I'd been so focused on Brad under the table that I didn't even see Gary walk in. Still holding onto Brad, he looked at me and said he got my message.

Struggling to pull away, Brad turned to me and yelled, "Who's this loser?"

Grabbing his other arm, Gary turned him so they were facing each other. He must have been gripping him hard because I saw Brad grimace. Looking him straight in the eyes, Gary answered, "I'm a friend of Gretchen's. You got a problem with that?"

Gary didn't release his hold on Brad as he looked at me and asked if I needed him to take me home. I shook my head *yes*, too upset to say anything. Gary shoved Brad away and told him he'd better leave me alone. Brad stood there for a second, looking like he might take a swing at Gary. Instead, he gave me a hateful look and stormed out the door.

By then I was trembling so badly, I could hardly stand. Gary asked if I was okay, and we sat down in the booth for a minute. I kept thanking him over and over for coming to help me. Once I calmed down a little, he asked, "Do you want to talk about what happened?"

I nodded and said, "I took your advice and told Brad we were finished. He told me we weren't finished until he said so, and he threatened to prove it to me when we got in his car. I was afraid to leave with him, so I called you."

"It's a good thing you did," Gary assured me. "Brad might've hurt you tonight to scare you into staying with him. I was worried when I couldn't get through to you on your cell. Why did you turn it off, anyway?"

"In case you tried to call me back," I explained. "I didn't want Brad to know that I'd called anyone for help."

Shaking his head, Gary said, "You should have left it on, Gretchen. Then you would've known I was on my way. Either way, you didn't have to leave with Brad tonight. You're in a public place, so he couldn't force you to go with him. All you had to do was refuse to get out of the booth and scream if he tried to make you. Someone here would've helped you. And the police would give you a ride home in a situation like this, I'm sure."

Looking at me, Gary saw that I felt pretty stupid about the way I'd handled things. Trying to console me, he added, "It was good you broke up with Brad somewhere in public, Gretchen, but you should've picked a safer place, like in the lobby of your sorority. Then you wouldn't have needed a ride home."

"I never thought about that," I admitted. "I only knew that I wanted my life back."

Smiling, Gary stood and helped me out of the booth. "Jesus wants you to have your life back, too. Let's get out of here and get you home."

On the drive back to campus, we talked about God and why we need Him in our lives every day. By the time we pulled up outside the house, I was ready to ask Jesus to be my Savior and Lord. Gary prayed with me, and I received Christ, right there in his car!

I reached out and gave Gretchen a big hug. "Oh, I'm so happy for you! You'll never be the same."

"To tell you the truth, I wanted to pray with Karen that day in The Coffee Cup, but I kept thinking that she wouldn't be asking me to accept Christ if she knew what I'd been doing with Brad. I didn't understand then that God accepts you based on what Jesus did for you when He died on the cross. I thought you had to be good enough to receive God's love and forgiveness.

"That's why when Brad stole my virginity, I just gave up and went along with him, feeling I could never be a whole person again. I believed that lie until Gary told me about how God forgave and accepted him—that gave me hope for myself. Now that I'm a child of God, I've never felt so complete!"

Gretchen's face was beaming, and I inwardly thanked God for giving her a brand new start. Suddenly, I remembered my intention to check with Carrie about Fran. I'd gotten so into Gretchen's story that I had forgotten all about my roommate. Just as I started to tell Gretchen that I needed to run down the hall for a minute, the door opened and Fran walked in.

"I'm so glad you're back!" I blurted out. "I was worried about you. Are you all right?"

"Yeah, just tired. I've been up all night talking with J.R. I'm pregnant, and neither of us knows what to do about it."

I couldn't believe she would come right out and say that with Gretchen in the room. However, she hadn't had any sleep and looked exhausted. She probably didn't care who knew at this point. Slipping out of her gown, Fran put on the jeans and T-shirt that were still lying on her bed and then sat down on her comforter.

Gretchen was the first to speak. "So, what did J.R. say when you told him you were pregnant?"

"He said we're too young to be parents. We both have two years of school left before we graduate, and neither of our families have a lot of money. Both of us have student loans, and J.R. says we can't afford the expense of a baby and still make it through school. He wants me to have an abortion."

"How do you feel about that?" Gretchen asked.

"Terrible!" she lamented, bursting into tears.

Both Gretchen and I were quickly at her side, trying to comfort her. After a few moments, Fran was ready to continue. "The problem is that I really love kids. I come from a family of eight, and I practically raised my younger sisters. I can't imagine ending a baby's life. I do agree with J.R. about one thing though—I'm not ready to make the sacrifices I saw my mom make for all of us.

"It's like there's no good solution for me. No matter what I do, I come out the loser. J.R. doesn't want to get married, so I'm on my own if I keep the baby. I'd have to quit school, get a job, and live with my parents. They still have kids of their own at home, and I know my mom. She won't be happy about helping to raise a grandchild at the same time. She's told me a million times that I'd better not let this happen.

"If I get an abortion, I know it will bother me for the rest of my life. I also run the risk that something could go wrong and ruin my chances to have a baby later on when I want children. I even thought about giving the baby up for adoption, but I don't think I can carry a child full term and then give it away.

"What really stinks is that J.R. can walk away from it all. I can't. It's like I'm in a bad dream that I can't wake up from. You know, in all the times J.R. and I had sex, we always used protection, except for once. I guess once is enough because I've taken three pregnancy tests, and all of them read positive. I keep hoping that between now and the end of school, J.R. will change his mind and help me work through this mess."

Gretchen put her arm around Fran. "I know how you feel."

"How could you?" Fran snapped back.

"Because it happened to me almost a year ago. Only I made the wrong choice; I let Brad pressure me into an abortion. You're right, Fran. It's something you never forget. The guy is just looking for an easy out, but there's nothing easy about this. The baby loses its life, but something inside of you dies, too. You'll regret what you've done for the rest of your life. I know I do. I would give anything to have the chance to make that decision again."

I shared my thoughts with Fran next. "All my life I was told that people shouldn't have sex outside of marriage. I just thought that was part of being a Christian. But I guess God tells us to be abstinent *for a reason*. It's not just a rule to keep us from having fun. God's trying to protect us from things like STDs and what you're facing right now, Fran. He knows that a good marriage is a safe place for sex. No fear. No guilt. You can enjoy it knowing you're loved and that your husband's committed to you for life, come what may. And when a couple does get pregnant, even if it's not an easy situation, they have each other for love and support to give that baby a solid home. God doesn't want us making choices that end up hurting us and others."

Gretchen nodded. "I'm not going to have sex again until I'm married."

Fran was surprised. "Brad won't like that."

"No problem there. I broke up with him for good after the dance."

Fran was so drained from being up all night that I suggested she get some sleep. Exhausted, she squirmed under her comforter and closed her eyes, now puffy and red from crying.

As Gretchen walked to the door, she turned to Fran and added, "After you get some rest, I have some new friends I want you to meet. Maybe they can help you work through this problem."

Fran was asleep before Gretchen finished her last sentence. We didn't want to disturb her, so we each went our separate ways. Gretchen left to go back to her room while I took a quick shower, got ready, and headed for the library.

Chapter 12

Walking Away

A brisk walk to the library was usually a good way to clear my head and work off stress. This time, however, it did nothing to make me feel better. I was happy for Gretchen, of course, but my mind kept replaying what had happened after the dance with Jay. I couldn't stop thinking about the look on his face when I refused his proposal; it still made me feel sick to my stomach.

Arriving at the library, I settled in at a table toward the back of the reference section. But no matter how hard I tried to concentrate on studying, my thoughts would inevitably return to Jay. He must have been thinking about me, too, because he found me working at my seat. "How's my girl to-day?" he asked light-heartedly.

His greeting irritated me. How was I going to make him understand that I couldn't be his girl? I didn't want to get into an argument, so I simply responded, "Fine. How did you know I was here?"

"I called your room and a sleepy-sounding Fran said you were out. I knew you had lots of studying to do this weekend; the library was a safe guess. So, have you thought any more about getting married?"

"No, Jay," I sighed. "I told you last night that I wasn't ready to marry anyone. I still have a lot of growing up to do."

"It's because I'm not a virgin, isn't it?"

"No! I just don't want to get married right now, okay? I want to finish college before I even think about being a wife. When I started dating you, it was my first time dating anyone. Then when we agreed to go out the second time, I thought we could hang out as friends and have some romance, too. But I forgot that people's feelings get involved. I never stopped to think that you were graduating this year and at a different stage in your life. You're ready for a permanent relationship; I'm not."

Jay was visibly frustrated. "I'm running out of ideas with you, Julia! I've stopped partying, and I've respected your decision to be a virgin, even though I want you so much. I read my Bible and go to church with you on Sundays. I even accepted Christ for you. I don't know what more you want!"

"You can't accept Christ for me, Jay; it's a relationship you have with Jesus. He's the reason for reading your Bible and going to church. You're supposed to do those things because you love and appreciate Him, not to please me. If getting me to date you again was your real motive for going down to the altar and asking Christ to be your Savior, you're not really a Christian. You're just acting out a role."

"Do you even know what you're talking about, Julia? Let me tell you what I know. I know that I love you and you love me, regardless of all your double talk. Your words don't speak as loud as your kisses; you have feelings for me, too."

"I never said I didn't. It's just that being attracted to someone isn't enough for what I want in a marriage."

"Then you need to tell the rest of the world! Why else should people get married, if not for love? All of this really comes down to one thing: you're afraid to let go and let yourself be happy."

I was fighting a losing battle, trying to appeal to Jay from a spiritual perspective. Karen had been right all along. I'd made a big mistake thinking I could have my romantic dream until school was out. All it did was give Jay hope for more. It was time to put an end to our relationship once and for all.

"Jay, this isn't getting us anywhere. It was a mistake thinking we could keep our feelings casual. I guess we couldn't. We need to stop seeing each other. It's not going to be any easier to say goodbye in ten days than it will today. In fact, it'll probably be a lot harder."

"Thanks, but I can handle it," he shot back, annoyed.

"I can't. I have to get my mind back on schoolwork. Finals are soon, and I need to do well on them to keep my scholarship. If you really care about me the way you say you do, you'll understand."

Standing up, I collected my books and looked at Jay for some kind of response. With a hurt expression, he simply said, "I hope you know you're walking away from a guy that really loves you." Pushing down feelings of guilt, I turned and left the library without another word.

When I arrived back at the house, I went upstairs and peeked into our room. Fran was still sleeping, so I walked down to one of the side rooms off the parlor to study. Laying out my books, I tried to concentrate on something other than Jay. Yet no matter how hard I tried, my mind kept drifting.

Ever since I could remember, I had wanted to be someone's girlfriend. Unfortunately, at both Jay's expense and mine, I found out that getting romantically involved can be really foolish if you're not ready. I learned that it's easy to fall in love with someone once you start spending time together. And it can happen even if you're not right for each other. But by that time, your emotions try to rule your decisions, and the choices you make are usually based more on feelings than rational thinking.

The pain that Jay and I were going through was much greater than the loneliness we'd experienced before dating. Jay said that I had feelings for him, and he was right. I did. That's what made walking away from him so hard, *even though I knew I'd made a mistake*. Once you've had a taste of what it's like to have a special someone in your life, the void that's left by his absence seems enormous.

Knowing how much I needed to study, I pried my thoughts away from my problems and tried to get focused again, which I managed to do for several hours. Then my stomach began growling, and I knew it was time for a break. Gathering up my things, I headed back to my room. Fran was awake by then and getting ready to go out. I wasn't quite sure what to say to her, so I simply asked, "Are you feeling any better?"

"I got some sleep while you were gone, but I'm not going to feel any better until J.R. comes up with a real solution. I can't believe this is even happening! It's such a nightmare. Sorry to be taking all this out on you, Julia. I know this is a happy time for you and Jay. He showed J.R. and me your engagement ring this week and told us how he was going to ask you to marry him after the dance. I'm sorry I forgot to congratulate you." Her eyes made their way to my finger. "Why aren't you wearing the ring?"

"I wouldn't accept it. I'm not ready to get married, Fran. I want to finish school first."

"Ironic, isn't it?" she mused. "Jay wants to marry you, but you aren't ready. I want to marry J.R., but he isn't ready. Maybe we're all crazy."

"No, I think we're all just immature and selfish. We want what we want now, and it ends up costing us and everybody else."

As she moved to the door, Fran gave me a faint smile. "I'm living proof of that. Wish me luck!"

Once she left, I called Gretchen's room to invite her to go to church with me in the morning. Her roommate said she went out to the movies with someone named Karen. I couldn't help but smile when I heard that. Gretchen was excited about being a new Christian and would be making lots of new friends as well. I was glad to be one of them. Since she was gone, I wrote a note and taped it to her door, asking her to be down at my room by quarter 'til nine the next morning if she wanted to go.

Karen would be expecting Jay and me to pick her up at the usual time for church. Only this Sunday, Jay wouldn't be riding with us. I dreaded telling Karen what had happened between Jay and me. It was going to be embarrassing to admit that I'd messed up *again*—that she'd been right all along.

The earlier growling in my stomach had grown into major hunger pangs, so I joined in with a bunch of girls who were ordering pizzas. Although school was winding down, study time was accelerating as finals approached. It was unusual to see this many girls in on a Saturday night. We were all making up for the time spent at the dance the night before.

When I was done eating, I read for a while and then tidied up my room. I was exhausted, more emotionally than physically. I desperately needed to turn off my thoughts and feelings—thoughts about how much I'd hurt Jay and feelings of loss because we wouldn't be seeing each other anymore. I knew that, in time, the hurt would go away for both of us. But that wasn't making the moment any more bearable. Sleep seemed to be my only escape, so I went to bed early.

When I woke up the next morning, I quietly got ready for church so Fran could sleep. As I slipped into the hallway and softly shut the door behind me, Gretchen was just coming down the hall. A few minutes later, we picked up Karen at her dorm. On the way to church, I explained to them what had happened with Jay and me. Karen was very gracious. She could've rubbed it in about not getting involved with him again, but she didn't.

I asked Gretchen if she'd heard from Brad since the scene at the restaurant. She said that he'd called her the night before, right after she'd gotten home from the movies. He told her he was sick of her anyway and that getting another girl would be easy.

Karen laughed when she heard that. "The truth is Gary showed up at Brad's frat house the morning after the dance and told him to stay away from you. He said that if anything happened to you, he'd be back—and not to talk. Brad didn't say much. Apparently, he only likes to push women around. He should leave you alone now."

Just as Karen finished her story, we pulled into the parking lot at church. It was already packed with cars, forcing us to find a space on one of the side streets. It took several minutes for us to walk to the building and make our way into the sanctuary. Worship had already begun, so we quickly found three seats near the back.

Gretchen seemed to be enjoying the message, but I felt edgy the whole time, wondering if Jay might come in late. I watched for him throughout the service, but he never showed up. Once we were back in the car, I breathed a sigh of relief. No more confrontations today at least! The three of us girls stopped for a quick bite to eat and then headed back to campus for another day of studying.

Chapter 13

One Last Date

The next few days were typical for the end of the term as students prepared for finals all over campus. They could be seen studying everywhere—at the library, in the student union, and out on the lawns.

Fran and J.R. were still trying to work out their problem, but no decision had been reached yet. Jay and I didn't cross paths again until the Wednesday following our breakup in the library. I was walking back to my house from class when I heard someone running up behind me. Looking back, I saw him chasing after me. "Julia, hold up a minute!" he shouted.

When he caught up, he was out of breath and had to pause for a moment before speaking. I stood there waiting, wondering what he'd say. After a few seconds, he was ready. "I got some great news today—my parents called and said they're flying here in time for graduation!"

Relieved that he only wanted to tell me about his parents, I smiled and told Jay how happy I was for him. He was grinning from ear to ear, a totally different man from the one I had left in the library a few days ago.

"Actually, they're arriving sometime Friday," he explained. "They have reserved a suite at the Eddington Hotel downtown. My dad made some business appointments in the area, and they plan to be here the whole week until graduation. They want me to stay with them so we can spend some time together before I leave for my job."

"That's great, Jay."

"I need a big favor from you, Julia. While we were dating, I talked to my parents about you a few times. They said on the phone that they want to meet you and take us both out for dinner Friday night. I couldn't tell them the truth about us. Not yet. I'll tell them next week that we broke up, but I want their first night here to be special. I really need you to do this for me."

In the past, I had hurt Jay because I was only thinking of myself. Looking at his expectant face, I felt obligated to make this happen for him. Reluctantly, I said, "Okay, Jay, I'll go."

"Thanks," he exhaled in relief. "I'll pick you up around seven. Make sure you dress up; my mother will want to go to the best restaurant she can find around here. I hope you like eating food with names you can't pronounce," he laughed. Thanking me again, he said a hurried goodbye and sprinted away. I looked at my watch and realized that he was already late for his three o'clock class.

As I watched him go, I suddenly regretted my decision, sorry I'd agreed to yet another date. Something just didn't feel right. I wanted to call to him and take it back, but it was too late; he was already out of sight. Sighing, I just shook off my concerns and continued my day.

When Thursday night rolled around, Gretchen came down to my room a bit early to show me the new Bible that Karen had given her. We both tried to get Fran to come with us to our final study group, but she was still on a mission with J.R.

We ran into some traffic on the drive over, making us arrive at the meeting a little late. Gary had already begun the lesson, so we quietly sat down, opened our Bibles, and tried to get into the message. I found myself looking over at Gretchen quite a bit, hoping she was getting something out of it. She was paying close attention and seemed to be touched by what was shared.

A few times during the evening, I felt like I should tell Karen about my Friday dinner date with Jay and his parents. But I just couldn't get the words out. I was embarrassed to admit that I was going to see him again.

Every time I thought my relationship with Jay was over, when I had just started to accept that fact and adjust my life accordingly, something always seemed to pull me back into being with him. It's not always easy to get back to where you should be. You get entangled in circumstances, and the people involved won't let you go without a struggle.

This time after the meeting, Gretchen did all the talking on the drive back to the sorority house. She was excited because Gary had promised to get her involved at his church back home during the summer. I didn't mention my date with Jay to Gretchen either. Again, I was embarrassed to admit it. "Why did I agree to go?" I kept asking myself. At the same time, I didn't have the heart to call Jay and back out. These last two weeks of school seemed to be taking an eternity to live out. All I wanted was to get the semester over with and go home.

When I got up the next morning, I still felt uneasy about my dinner date with Jay. That feeling gnawed at me all day, but I figured it was probably because I was sort of sneaking out with him without telling anyone. I hadn't planned to tell Fran, either, but she was getting ready to go out with J.R. at the same time I was dressing. By my dress and high heels, it was obvious I was going somewhere special. I wasn't surprised when she asked me where I was going.

At first, I was tempted to make up something, but I decided that if my life of lies was ever going to end, it might as well be right then. "I'm helping Jay out tonight. His parents are in town early for his graduation, and we are meeting them at the Eddington before going out to dinner. Jay begged me to do this for him; I couldn't say no."

I expected some kind of lecture to follow, but all Fran said was, "Oh, that's nice. Have fun." Then she put on some lip gloss and was out the door. For a moment, I was disappointed that she hadn't tried to talk me out of going. Then I remembered that it was *Fran* I was talking to; for her, there were no absolutes in a relationship—just do what you want and have a good time.

When I went downstairs at seven, Jay was already waiting for me. "Wow, you look beautiful. Thanks for coming tonight."

"That's okay. I just don't want to be out too late, Jay. I need to study all weekend for my finals next week, and I want to get an early start in the morning."

"No problem," he assured me. "You'll be in bed early tonight, I promise."

The drive over to meet his parents was uncomfortable; Jay was acting like we'd never broken up. When he reached for my hand as usual, I reminded myself that I only had to get through this one last date for his parents' sake, and then I would finally be free.

The Eddington had valet parking. I felt like a celebrity when we pulled up to the front and a doorman helped me out of the car. Inside, the hotel lobby was decorated with marble pillars, plush carpeting, and huge crystal chandeliers. Jay led me over to a velvet couch and asked me to sit down while he called his parents' room to see if they were ready.

Soon he returned with a smile. "My mother needs ten more minutes before we come up; they're not quite dressed yet. She said room service just delivered some hors d'oeuvres, but I have an idea. Stay here. I'll be right back." I watched him disappear into the restaurant across the lobby. Several minutes later, he made his way back to me with a cup in each hand. "How about a final cappuccino together?"

"Never turn one down," I grinned, taking mine from him.

It was the perfect temperature for drinking, and I quickly finished it. I hadn't eaten anything since early morning and was looking forward to the hors d'oeuvres that were waiting for us in his parents' room. When Jay had emptied his cup, he suggested we head upstairs. "I can't wait to see which restaurant in this town stood up against my mother's scrutiny," he said, rolling his eyes.

We were laughing as we entered the elevator. Reaching in front of me, Jay pushed the appropriate button, and we zipped straight up to the ninth floor. When the elevator came to a stop, I suddenly felt dizzy. As we exited, I was cradling my head with one hand and grasping Jay's arm with the other.

He looked concerned. "Are you all right?"

"I'm fine. I just haven't had much to eat today, and I'm feeling kind of weak."

"You'll feel better once we get some food into you," he said.

I was anxious to meet Jay's mom to see if she was as snobbish as her son portrayed her to be. We walked quite a distance down the hall before he finally stopped and took out a room key card. As he unlocked the door, I felt dizzy again and almost collapsed. Pushing the door open, Jay caught me in his arms and lifted me off my feet.

"Put me down," I whispered. "What will your parents think?"

His answer stunned me. "I understand it's customary to carry the bride over the threshold."

"That's not funny!" I scolded in a hushed voice.

Kicking the door closed behind him, he carried me over to a couch and set me down. By then I was starting to get very drowsy. Something was definitely wrong. A feeling of panic swept over me, and I cried, "Where are your parents, Jay?"

"They're not here, Julia. This suite is for us. I've been going out of my mind the past few days trying to come up with a way to keep you in my life. I can't let you walk away from me. I love you and need you, and I know you love me, too. Everything will work out fine after tonight."

It took all my strength to push out, "Please take me home…"

Kneeling down beside me, he took my hand. "After tonight, you won't want to go home. I know you, Julia, how important your virginity is to you. You said it yourself: it's a gift you can only give once and to one person. I'm just sorry I don't have a gift for you. But I promise I'll make it up to you for giving it away before we met."

I kept crying out for my body to fight back, to resist what was happening to me, but it could no longer obey my commands. The drug Jay had put in my cappuccino had sapped all my strength. As I listened to him, his words came crashing over me like waves over a drowning person. I was aware of every one, but powerless to stop my impending fate.

Jay picked me up and carried me into the bedroom. When he stood me up and unzipped my dress, I felt it drop to the floor. Once again my knees buckled, and he quickly caught me and lifted me onto the bed. Somehow I perceived that he was undressing. His voice continued reaching to me as though it were far off in the distance. "Tomorrow we'll talk about getting married, Julia. We're having our wedding night a little early, that's all. That's why I got the bridal suite for you."

I wanted to beg Jay not to do this terrible thing, to cry out to Jesus to forgive and help me, but I couldn't speak. When I felt him climb into bed next to me, I could barely hear Jay as he whispered in my ear, "I'm going to make love to you now, Julia. When you wake up in my arms, you'll finally see that we belong together."

As he pressed his lips against mine, I felt as if I were floating backwards into a deep, dark cavern where there was a strange pounding. Then I faintly heard a man's voice calling to Jay. But I couldn't tell where the voice was coming from or if what I heard was even real. It seemed to be somewhere in the background, floating along with me. Unable to stay awake any longer, I let go and allowed sleep to overtake me.

Chapter 14

Heavenly Assistance

When I regained consciousness, I was lying in a hospital bed. My parents were standing over me, praying. At first I couldn't believe what I was seeing. Then my mom looked up and saw I was awake. In tears, she sat down on the bed and pulled me close. "Look, Phil, we've got our Julia back!"

Leaning down, my dad cupped my face in his hand. "You gave us a real scare there, honey. Thank God you're okay."

For the next few minutes, none of us said much. We were too busy hugging and kissing one another. Once we all settled down, I began to fire questions at them. "How did I get here? How did *you* get here? Where's Jay? Did he…?"

My dad interrupted me. "One question at a time, Julia. First of all, you're here because of a drug overdose. When they called us, your mom and I caught the first plane out. Then they picked us up at the airport and brought us to the hospital. And no, Julia, Jay didn't rape you. They got there in time."

I was overwhelmed with both relief and gratitude. Jesus had heard my desperate, silent cry for help in that hotel room. Somehow He'd found a way to save me at the very last minute. I was bursting to know who had come to my rescue.

"Who are the *they* you keep talking about?" I asked, mystified.

"Some very good friends," my mom replied. "They're down the hall waiting to see you."

My dad left the room for a minute. When he returned, Gary, Gretchen, Fran, Kenny, and Karen followed him in through the door. Then the hugging started all over again, followed by a few tears of joy. Finally, I couldn't stand the suspense any longer. "How did you guys know? What happened? How did I get here?"

My dad grinned. "She likes to ask questions in multiples."

Fran was the first to speak. "Remember when I left ahead of you to meet J.R.? Well, while we were driving in the car, I mentioned to him how nice you looked and that you were going with Jay to the Eddington to meet his parents. J.R. laughed and said that Jay's parents were still overseas and that he was taking you to the Eddington to introduce you to more than his mom and dad.

"I knew what he meant, so when we stopped for gas a few minutes later, I made up an excuse to go inside. Then I pulled out my cell and called Gretchen. Luckily, she was in her room. I told her what J.R. had said and that I thought you were headed for trouble. She said not to worry; she had a plan."

"I'll take it from here," Gretchen offered. "When Fran told me what she thought was going on, I was really afraid for you, Julia. I called Gary right away, catching him and Kenny as they were leaving his apartment."

Jumping in, Gary said, "Gretchen told me what she suspected and where you were. I wanted her to go with us, but I didn't want to take time to swing by and pick her up. Instead, I told her to try to get her own ride to the hotel."

"That's when I got involved," Karen inserted. "Gretchen called me and asked if I could pick her up. I was there in ten minutes, and we left for the Eddington, too."

Gary continued, "We arrived just ahead of the girls and ran up to the man working the front desk. I explained that a girl might be in trouble in the hotel and asked if a guy named Jason Wells was registered. He told me he was in room 920 and slid a key card across the counter toward me. I was shocked he'd do that, but I wasn't going to question it.

"Kenny grabbed the key, and we bolted for the elevator. A minute later we were on the ninth floor, sprinting down the hall, praying we weren't too late. As soon as we found the right room, I started pounding on the door. When no one an-

swered, Kenny used the key to get in. I could tell
the bedroom was a separate room off to the right,
so I shouted to Jay and told him to get to his feet,
that we were coming in."

Karen continued. "Gretchen and I were right
behind the guys. We barely had a chance to ask the
man at the desk what we wanted before he told us
we were looking for room 920. Then he pointed to
the elevators on the far side of the lobby, and we
jetted upstairs. When we found the room, the door
was wide open. As soon as we ran in, Kenny asked
us to cover you with a blanket. Jay had his pants
on by then, and Gary had him pushed up against
the wall."

Kenny was eager to tell what happened next.
"I went over to the bed to try to get some kind of
response from you, but you were unconscious. I
could tell you'd been drugged. When I asked Jay
what he'd given you, he had no idea. One of the
guys at his frat house had given something to him,
saying it was safe. You didn't look right, and I was
afraid of an overdose. I told Karen to call 911."

Gary picked it up from there. "Jay kept swear-
ing to all of us that he never meant to hurt you,
that he loved you and wanted to marry you. I guess
he didn't get that it takes two people to make that
decision. I was so mad I wanted to knock him
through a wall. Instead, I shoved him out of the
suite and into the hallway, locking him out.

"When the paramedics arrived, they checked your pulse and breathing and confirmed the overdose. They quickly wheeled you to the ambulance and let Karen ride in the back with you to the hospital."

"I prayed like crazy the whole way!" Karen cried. "It was so scary, Julia."

"The rest of us rode with Gary," Gretchen chimed in. "On the way to the hospital, I looked in your purse and found an insurance card with your dad's name and number on it. I called right away on my cell."

"We received her call around nine," my mom said. "Your dad got us on the next flight out, and Gary and Kenny picked us up at the airport. We were here at the hospital by two a.m. When we talked to the doctor, he told us that you were a pretty sick girl, but it looked like your condition had stabilized. He felt confident that you would be okay. All we could do was wait for you to wake up."

"So, how did you get here, Fran?" I asked. "Weren't you with J.R. this whole time?"

Fran was anxious to get back into the conversation. "Are you kidding? I was so mad at J.R. that I made him take me back to the sorority house. I found Theresa and borrowed her car to drive to the Eddington. When I got there, I found out that a girl had been taken to the hospital. Then I drove here and found Gretchen and your friends in the waiting room."

"Gary, tell her about Daryl," Gretchen urged. "This is too weird, Julia—wait 'til you hear."

"Okay," Gary agreed. "After Kenny and I brought your parents to the hospital, we were told there was nothing to do but wait. That was driving me crazy, so I volunteered to go pick up Karen's car that was still at the Eddington. Kenny drove me over so I could bring her car back here. When I got to the hotel, I decided to go inside and thank that guy Daryl for helping us.

"When I walked into the lobby, a woman was working the front desk. She told me she had come on duty at midnight. When I asked if I could leave a note for Daryl, she said, 'Daryl who?' I described him to her, but she just smiled at me as though I were joking. She then informed me that they had no one working the front desk named Daryl. I told her that she had to be wrong because I read his name tag when he gave me the key. She still insisted that he was not an employee of the hotel."

"How do you explain that, Julia?" Gretchen cried, her eyes sparkling with delight. "Your mom thinks he was an angel sent by God to help you!"

"It may have been our prayers that got you some heavenly assistance," my dad remarked. "After dinner last night, your mom suddenly looked at me and said we had to pray for you right then, that she sensed you were in trouble. I have learned to trust your mom's instincts, so we stopped what we were doing and started praying for you. We'd just finished when Gretchen's call came in."

There was one more question I had to ask. "What happened to Jay?"

"I didn't kill him, if that's what you mean," my dad said angrily. "He's still waiting in the lobby for a report on you. He said he wouldn't leave until you were awake and he knew you would be all right. I told him he couldn't see you again, Julia, for any reason, not even to apologize. He lost that right when he hurt you the way he did."

"I don't know how to thank all of you," I expressed tearfully. "I'm ashamed of the way I've handled everything. I hope you can forgive me."

"We do forgive you, Julia," my dad replied. "We're all just grateful that you're safe. Everything else can be worked out."

"Julia needs to rest now," my mom decided. "You can see her later."

Everyone took a turn giving me a hug and saying goodbye. Fighting back tears, I realized what great friends I had. When I was finally alone with my parents, I asked if I could *please* get something to eat. I was hungry enough to eat anything, including hospital food.

My dad smiled before starting for the door. "I'll let your mom take care of that. I've got to go downstairs and tell Jay the danger is over, that you're okay. By the way, the hospital reported your overdose to the police. They want to know if you're going to press charges against Jay for what he did to you. You're over eighteen, so the decision is yours."

"Do I have to decide right now, Dad? My mind's all jumbled and confused. I know what he did was wrong, but I knew Jay's feelings for me were getting out of control, and I kept ignoring all the warning signs."

"I'm aware of that, honey. When you've eaten and rested, we are going to have a long talk."

Once he had gone, my mom called the nurse and asked her to bring me a tray. It came with only broth and Jell-O, but to me it was heaven. The nurse said she would order something more later, once she checked with the doctor. He came in about a half an hour later and gave us a glowing report.

"I never expected you to be doing this well so soon," he said, pleased. "I think you can handle some real food for dinner. I'll be sure to leave word at the nurses' station. If you continue at this rate, I'll release you to go home in the morning."

Once we had both thanked the doctor, he excused himself to go look in on some other patients. After he left, my mom insisted that I settle down and rest. I didn't argue. I was beginning to feel very drowsy, either from the drug that was still in my system or from the sheer relief of having my secret life exposed and forgiven. Regardless, I was asleep in a matter of minutes.

Chapter 15

Necessary Consequences

M y much-needed slumber was interrupted when one of the nurses came in to check on me. As she hurried off to continue her rounds, I rolled over to find my father sitting in a chair near the window. Looking up from the book he was reading, he greeted me with his usual smile.

"Hi, Dad," I said, still a bit groggy. "How long did I sleep?"

"A few hours. Did you have a good nap?"

"Uh huh," I answered, yawning. "Where's Mom?"

"I checked us into a hotel near campus and sent her over there to get some rest," he explained. "She'll be back soon."

Hearing a distant rattling in the hall, I knew the dinner trays were coming. My stomach was growling, but before I could eat, I had to use the bathroom. Timing it perfectly, I crawled back in bed just as my tray arrived. I don't remember what they brought me, but whatever it was, I ate every crumb.

When I was finished eating, my dad came over and sat down next to me on the bed. I knew it was time for our father-daughter talk. He smiled and gently took my hand. "I think you know how much your mom and I love you, Julia. We want you to know that we're not disappointed in you as our daughter, only with some of the choices you've made since coming to college.

"All kids look forward to becoming an adult and managing their own lives. But being successful at it has nothing to do with age, Julia. It has everything to do with our ability to make good decisions for ourselves and others.

"When your mom and I agreed to let you come to Tyler, it was a big step for all of us. We have always tried to give you as much freedom as you could handle, and we felt you were mature enough to go away to school. We weren't happy about sending you to a college so far away from home, but you had your heart set on coming here, and we wanted to make this happen for you. But now, in view of what you've been through, I think we need to make some changes.

"While we were driving from the airport to the hospital, I had a long talk with Gary. He told me about being your study group leader, what he thought was going on with you here at school. He felt that even though you wanted to be a Christian when you came to Tyler, you also wanted to do things you saw other students doing—nothing seriously wrong, just some things you weren't allowed to do at home.

"What concerned him most was the way you would go to the study group meetings and church on Sundays, but still make decisions that you knew weren't right. He told me that you weren't open and honest with your Christian friends about what was going on in your life, like moving into the sorority house, lying to us, and repeatedly dating Jay. He felt you resisted any accountability, that you wanted to do your own thing without your friends or family knowing. When it didn't work out, you would apologize, only to turn around and make the same mistake again.

"There's a word for that kind of behavior, Julia. *Immaturity.* It's still hard for me to believe that you lied to us about moving into the sorority house, working so hard to make us think you were still in the dorm. You managed to fool everyone somewhere along the way. Except your mom, that is. She sensed that something was wrong when she could never reach you at the dorm. She knew that you weren't acting like yourself. I thought she was just overreacting to having you gone for the first time. I'll never doubt her intuitions again.

"When you honestly look back on all that's happened to you this semester, you need to ask yourself what finally rescued you from your double life and all the pain that went along with it. The answer is that you finally planted a seed God was able to use.

"When you were honest with Fran about where you were going with Jay and why, a nugget of truth was planted like a seed. Then that seed was able to produce a crop—or plan—to rescue you. Fran mentioned your date to her boyfriend, which brought out what Jay was really planning. Then that truth was shared with others who loved you enough to act when they knew you were in trouble.

"If you hadn't told Fran the truth when you did, Jay would've raped you, Julia. And that would have been *his* fault, *his* crime. But even so, the pain of it would have been yours. And you would've had to work through it even though Jay was to blame.

"You must realize that the truth releases God to work for you. Lies don't. And until I see that you're capable of making better choices, I'm going to have to act as your father and help you. I want to share with you some of the decisions I've made so far.

"You will not be going back to the sorority house when you leave the hospital. I want you out of that environment immediately. I've rented a car and a trailer, and I plan to go to your room tomorrow, load up all your stuff, and take it home. I'll leave whatever clothes and personal things you need to get through the next week. Your mom will stay here with you at the hotel until you're finished with your final exams. Then you two can drive your car home.

"I've told Jay that he's not to try to see you before you leave on Friday. I want that guy permanently out of your life. I don't trust him—neither should you. Can I trust you not to contact him?"

"Of course, Dad. I really learned my lesson this time. I don't trust him either. More than anything, I don't trust myself around him. He's such a liar and can obviously make me believe whatever he wants. He made me think he had changed and become a Christian. Do you think he really did?"

My dad tried to be as objective as he could under the circumstances. "There's no way any of us could know that, Julia. The spiritual birth that Jesus talks about in the Bible takes place inside of a person. It happens when someone asks Christ for forgiveness and accepts His death on the cross to pay for their sins. Only God knows for sure when it happens. All we can do is wait to see good fruit in a person's life as evidence of a real change. I personally don't think Jay did accept Christ; his fruit was rotten."

I had to ask one more question. "Do you think Jay was really in love with me?"

My dad paused and thought before answering. "I would have to say that Jay loved you in a limited way, Julia. Without God in his life, a man often loves a woman based on what she does for him: how she makes him feel or how she meets a need in his life. But that's a selfish kind of love. And one that's subject to change. But Christ inside a man can help him love you sacrificially, the way Christ loves the Church.

"Jay saw you as his savior, Julia. He thought his relationship with you would fill the void in his life. That's why he fought so hard to keep you with him. When he knew he was losing you for good, he got desperate. Desperate people do desperate things. But real love wouldn't cause someone to do what Jay did to you.

"I want to explain something to you, sweetheart. When God placed you in our family almost nineteen years ago, He put you under my leadership. But I never *owned* you. I just had the responsibility to care for and protect you, as well as lead you into a personal relationship with God. And I'll continue to care for and protect you until the day I walk you down the aisle and place your hand in the hand of your husband.

"Somewhere in this world there's a young man depending on me to deliver you safely to his side. After you're married, it will then be his responsibility to continue to care for and protect you. But he won't own you either. All Christians belong only to Christ because He's the one who paid the price of His blood to purchase us.

"I came too close to blowing my responsibility to God Friday night. You were just seconds away from being raped, and if your friends hadn't gotten you to the hospital when they did, you might have lost your life. I'm not going to let that happen again.

"Gary told me that the Bible study group began praying for you when they found out you'd moved into the sorority house. And Karen told us that Jay had tried to force himself on you once before in his car. They all thought you had broken off your relationship with him for good.

"But instead, you continued to get caught up in Jay's life. He acted like he'd received Christ, so you went against godly advice and started seeing him again. Sensing that something was wrong, your mom began praying an hour every day for you and repeatedly tried to get you to confide in her, but you refused.

"What I'm getting at, Julia, is this: you can't depend on the prayers of other people to bail you out of negative situations the rest of your life. Angelic visitations aren't common, and neither are guys like Gary who are willing to go to such lengths to help others. The Bible warns us that we will reap what we sow. The next time you refuse to use the wisdom God gives you, there may be nobody there to rescue you.

"In view of all that's happened, your mom and I have decided that some necessary consequences are in order. You won't be coming back to Tyler next term, honey. It's foolish for us to pay for something that could end up hurting you. We have a college back home where you can earn your degree. Your mistakes have shown us that you need more time to mature before being totally out on your own. From now on, the men in your life are going to have to answer to me for the way they treat you."

Finished with what he had to say, my dad gave me a chance to respond. By then I was so choked up, I could hardly speak. I just threw my arms around his neck and released months of pent-up emotion. Choking on tears, I finally said, "I never meant to hurt you and Mom. I'm so sorry for everything I've done. I don't care about coming back here next year. I'm ready to go home." My dad didn't say a word. He simply held and comforted me like he had all my life.

My mom walked in while he was still holding me. "Looks like you two have everything worked out," she said with a smile as she brought over a box of tissues. We both nodded as I wiped my tears.

The doctor released me the next morning, so my mom picked me up in my car and took me straight to the hotel. My dad was already moving my things out of the sorority house by then. He wanted to get on the road early to get back home in time to prepare for a court appearance he had on Monday. Knowing that I had to make up for lost study time, my mom had transferred my books to the hotel room.

By noon, my dad had all my things packed and ready to go. He brought lunch in to us at the hotel so we could have some family time and pray together before he had to leave. Once he was gone, my mom and I stayed in as I prepared for exams.

We had room service deliver dinner so I could finish studying and get some rest before my two finals the following day.

The next morning, my mother dropped me off at Tyler. Then she went to the mall to kill time during my exams, picking me up when I was done. After a nice lunch, we headed back to the hotel again. I had two more finals on Wednesday and then nothing else until Friday afternoon.

When we got back to our room, my mom pulled out a new book she had bought, and I studied. We agreed to read and study the rest of the day before dressing up and going out for dinner. Time sped by. It was fun getting ready together and deciding where to go to eat. I wanted Italian food, so we looked in the phone book to find a restaurant near our hotel.

It had been so long since I had my mom all to myself, mainly because my brother John had gotten married the previous summer. For almost a year, planning both his wedding and my graduation took up much of our time. Then my parents and I got all caught up in getting me ready for college in the fall.

Spending time with my mom at the hotel made me remember the special relationship there had always been between us. She was more than just my mom; she was one of my closest friends. Foolishly, I had forgotten that over the last semester.

Chapter 16

Girl Talk

We found the restaurant with no problem, and after a short wait, the hostess seated us at a booth in the back of the dining room. Once we had ordered, the waitress brought out a small platter of antipasto as an appetizer, which we devoured in a matter of minutes. During the meal, my mom and I chatted away as though nothing bad had happened. But by dessert, I was ready to share some of the feelings I was still working through regarding Jay.

"Mom, is it all right to talk about what happened?" I began sheepishly.

"Of course," she assured me with a smile.

"There are so many things I don't understand," I admitted. "Actually, it's not so much about Jay; it's more about me. How could I turn my back on you and Dad and my friends the way I did? As a Christian, how could I let myself get involved in this mess? Why did I do so many foolish things when I knew better?"

"Your dad was right; you do like to ask questions in multiples," my mom laughed. "I guess we should begin by recognizing that you made a lot of wrong choices, honey. But before we answer your *how could I* questions, let's start with the *why* one. Knowing why you did something helps you avoid making the same mistake again. Let's back up and examine the first wrong choice you can remember making."

I thought for a moment. "It was the one I made to join the sorority and move in there without telling you."

"Okay, so why did you make that choice? What was the real reason behind it?"

"To be honest, I joined the sorority because I was tired of not having any fun. I wanted to go to parties and dances like other girls, and I was hoping to meet a Christian guy and finally have a boyfriend of my own."

My mom pulled out a pen and notebook from her purse and wrote down the reasons I had just given. I knew I was in for one of her extended lessons, but this time I was willing to listen.

"You just gave me several reasons for that first choice," she noted. "I have a feeling there's a common thread running through all of them. We'll try to find it by looking at each of your reasons separately. The first thing you said was that you were tired of not having any fun. That tells me you felt restricted in your Christian life. You wanted something that wasn't being offered to you at home, church, or in your Bible study group.

"Next you said you wanted to go to parties and dances. I assume that meant going there with a date. Which leads us to the last reason: you were hoping to meet a Christian guy and have a boyfriend of your own. And that meant going places where you could meet more guys. Sorority life was your chance, right?"

"Right, only none of it worked out," I conceded.

"That's because it was doomed to fail, Julia. But it's important that you know *why* it failed. Tell me, once you got involved in the sorority, what were the parties you went to like? Did you meet a lot of Christians there?"

I was sure she already knew the answers to those questions, but I answered her anyway. "The parties had a lot of drinking and stuff, and while there may have been some other Christians there, I didn't meet any."

"Okay, how did you feel about living in the house and going to those types of parties?"

"Well, I was uncomfortable with the language and drinking, and I basically felt out of place. I also learned that a lot of the girls were working through major problems with their boyfriends. Dating wasn't all fun like I'd thought."

"So sorority life wasn't what you expected. What happened next?"

"After living in the house about a month, I decided I didn't belong there. I couldn't go back to the dorm since I'd already paid for the semester, so I just stopped going to those parties and went back to my Bible study group."

"At the same time, what were you still hoping to do?"

We sang out the answer together: "*Meet a Christian guy.*"

My mom posed the next logical question. "Would Christian guys like Gary look for a girl-friend at your kind of sorority?"

"Probably not," I acknowledged.

"So basically, you went to the wrong place to find a boyfriend. You went somewhere where people who are living for God aren't easy to find, someplace where physical attraction is the number one reason for dating. Think about it, Julia. You're a beautiful girl. A guy sees you and wants to date you, but he finds out that you only date Christians. Now you're a challenge to his ego. He will become whatever he thinks you want to eventually get from you what he wants.

"You were so driven to have a boyfriend that you were willing to accept the first guy who came along claiming to be a Christian. The trap was set. Unfortunately, Jay got caught in his own trap because he ended up falling in love with you.

"In your first question, you asked how you could turn your back on Dad and me and the friends you'd made in your study group. The answer is that we weren't providing a boyfriend for you. In fact, we seemed to be keeping you from finding one. That's why you stopped telling us the truth about what you were doing. We became the enemy toward achieving your goal. And when things didn't work out like you thought they would, you were embarrassed to tell us that you'd made a mistake, pushing you even farther away from us.

"Let's go on to your second question: How could you allow yourself as a Christian to get involved in such a mess? The answer is that you started compromising what you knew was right. Always remember: God's ways are designed to help and bless you; compromising them will eventually invite problems into your life.

"The flaw in your plan was expecting to find a mature Christian guy in that environment. Maybe you were so tired of waiting for romance, you were secretly willing to accept a counterfeit. As long as he looked and acted like a Christian, you wouldn't have to feel guilty about dating him."

Everything she said was true, and I knew it. I didn't want to hold anything back; I wanted to be completely honest.

"Mom, I have to tell you something that's been bothering me. When I first started dating Jay, I knew deep down that he was not a Christian. Even so, I had real feelings for him. We had fun together, and I loved it when he held and kissed me, except for the times he lost control. Toward the end, I was convinced that he *had* become a Christian. Yet when he asked me to marry him, I didn't want to. How could I have feelings of love for him and not want to marry him?"

"Because, honey, most of what you felt for Jay was infatuation. You were in love with *being in love*, and then Jay came along. I saw him at the hospital; he's really handsome! When he held and kissed you, it was thrilling to your senses. But you were only looking for a romantic adventure, not a permanent relationship. Dating Jay hadn't demanded much from you until he offered marriage. Suddenly, you realized you weren't ready to make that kind commitment."

"That scares me, Mom. What if I'm never ready? How will I know?"

"If you cooperate with God, you'll be ready. You'll know it's the right time and the right person because He'll tell you. Your problem was that you got ahead of God's plan for you. God does not cause confusion, Julia. He won't bring a man into your life before you're ready to accept the responsibilities that go with that relationship."

"Please help me understand, Mom. If I'm not ready for God to bring my mate into my life, why do I feel this constant aching inside for a boyfriend? Why was I so miserable before I met Jay? Honestly, I was getting depressed about it. Why do I feel even more miserable now that I've done the right thing and broken it off with him?"

"The answers to those questions are complex, Julia. Do you really want to hear them?"

"I think I *need* to hear them," I replied with a wry smile.

My mom smiled back, reached over, and gave my hand a squeeze. "You know the Bible tells us that God is love. Well, since we've been made in His image, we're only complete when we know we're unconditionally loved and accepted. Our parents do their best to give us the love we need as children, but as we mature, their imperfect love is no longer enough. We begin to crave a more meaningful, intimate relationship that only God Himself can provide. It's only when we learn to love, fear, and serve the Lord that we're truly satisfied. It's His love we need more than anything.

"But the enemy tries to convince us that our deepest needs can be met through another person. He lies and says that romance will fulfill us, make us truly happy. He uses media to bombard us with unrealistic expectations about being in love.

"God does want us to experience love and all the joy that comes with being joined to another person. But He has to be our *first love*; only He can completely fulfill us.

"You said that you felt an aching inside for a boyfriend. That's normal. Before I met your dad, I felt the same thing. That longing comes to get you ready for your husband. Understanding that will make it easier for you to deal with the pain of waiting.

"As women, we can expectantly watch for our man, but we don't have to go out on a crusade to find him. We can trust God for both the right person and the divinely scheduled time to meet him.

God knows better than we do the *who*, *when*, and *why*. And He has promised to work everything out for our good.

"In the meantime, Julia, you need to find yourself in Christ, to discover the gifts and callings He's placed within you. Take time to develop a close friendship with God before anything else. Remember, He designed marriage as a supplement to, not a substitute for, your relationship with Him.

"Be patient, Julia. Allow God the freedom to match you up with the right man so your spiritual lives can flow together. He will make sure that your gifts and talents complement each other. Best of all, your lives will be filled with peace instead of conflict.

"When you know there will be a lapse between the time you start wanting a mate and the time you finally meet him, you won't be as tempted to panic. The delay causes an appreciation to develop within your heart—and you'll be less likely to take him for granted. It's never fun to wait for something you really want. Exercising patience does cost you. But it's always worth it. *He's* worth it! So, while you're waiting for Mr. Right, learn through your relationships with other people how to serve and be a blessing in someone else's life.

"Other than God, your marriage relationship will be the most important one in your life. That's why the enemy will do anything to stop God's plan to bring you together with the right person.

"A lot of movies, books, and TV shows glamorize romance. The more you feed on those things, the more the void you have in your heart for someone expands. Eventually, the natural longing God put there is replaced with lust. Lust isn't always sexual. Lust is simply when you start to feel an overwhelming desire to have or experience something.

"That's what happened to you, Julia. Having a boyfriend became an obsession. Nothing else could satisfy you. The one thing you didn't have became the only thing you wanted. That made it easy for the enemy to set you up with a counterfeit. Remember that a counterfeit looks and feels like the real thing; it just has no real or lasting value.

"Romance is a beautiful part of love, but by itself, it's not a lasting foundation for a marriage. Once the initial excitement begins to wear off, you're left with two people who each have flaws and weaknesses.

"The only sure foundation for marriage is God's kind of love, which is based on covenant—a commitment that will cause you to stay in the relationship even when things get difficult. That takes a high level of maturity. You discovered something with Jay: what you wanted and thought you couldn't live without ended up being something you weren't ready to handle.

"You said the void you felt was even stronger now that your relationship with Jay is over. That's another price you pay for getting ahead of God's timing. Before dating Jay, you only imagined what it must be like to have a boyfriend. Now you know the fun of having someone to go places with and the thrill of being kissed. It's perfectly natural that you're feeling a greater loss."

"Okay, Mom. I understand everything you're saying, but I'm still confused. You and Dad didn't want me to date in high school, and my experience with Jay here at college was a disaster. Obviously, I don't' know what I'm doing, and I have no idea where to go from here. How is dating supposed to work?"

"I don't blame you for being confused, Julia. Our society seems just as confused when it comes to premarital relationships. When I get perplexed about an issue, I always try to find principles in the Bible that can help my understanding.

"The first thing you need to realize is that dating as we know it is not modeled in Scripture. In Biblical times, most marriages were arranged. But in our Western culture, there's a lot of pressure to have a boyfriend as early as middle school and high school. Even some Christians do a lot of dating before finally getting married. But doing that when you're not mature enough to handle those relationships can cause a lot of heartache for everyone involved.

"The Bible doesn't give us set rules for the dating issues we face today. Yet it does give some basic principles regarding relationships between men and women. All I can do is share my opinion with you, which is based on what I've learned through my own study and experience.

"Let's start where a relationship begins. We'll call it the *discovery stage*. When you meet a man for the first time, you form an impression of him. If it's a good one, you'll naturally want to know more about him. During this early stage, everything is new and exciting; expectations are high. If things go well, you'll probably want to get to know each other better and move into stage two.

"Stage two involves developing a friendship. To do that, you begin spending time together, sometimes in a group or maybe just the two of you. It's in this stage that you start to see whether you match up. Do you laugh and have a good time together? Do you enjoy many of the same things? Do you communicate well? Having someone to do things with meets a companionship need in your life, and if you're not under any pressure romantically, you can relax and just be yourself.

"Never skip the *friendship stage*, Julia. You're using this time to take a man's spiritual temperature. Is he hot, cold, or lukewarm? It takes time to read his commitment to God, so take things slow. Being attracted to him physically doesn't mean that you're matched spiritually.

"Try to keep things on a friendship level as long as you can. Remember, friends just hang out together and have fun. They don't act like boyfriend and girlfriend. As soon as you start holding hands and kissing, it becomes much harder to stay objective and honestly evaluate each other. Find out how well you relate as a couple before you go any further.

"Be careful what signals you're sending a man. Teasing, flirting, and indiscreet clothing are all a real come on. You may only be trying to have some fun and get a little attention, but he's dealing with some strong passion issues. Don't light a fire that has no place to burn. If you do, you might be the one to get burned.

"Here's another tip about the friendship stage. When a guy is showing interest in you, he usually has more than friendship in mind. He probably has plenty of friends he can hang out with; he's spending time and money on you because he's looking for a girlfriend. He'll be willing to play the friendship game for a while hoping you'll eventually fall for him.

"So, if you see that a guy is starting to have feelings for you that you can't return, let him down gently but firmly. The longer you wait, the more he'll get hurt. You don't have to love a man just because he's interested in you.

"There will come a time when you've been seeing someone for a while and you both want more than friendship. Now you're ready for the *pre-engagement stage* of your relationship. This is when you start seriously considering one another as a marriage partner.

"Romance usually starts to enter the picture here, but you have to realize that showing affection will cause strong emotional ties to form. That's why sex is forbidden outside of marriage. It makes you completely vulnerable to the other person, *one flesh*, the Bible says. Where there is this kind of intimacy, there needs to be a lifetime marriage covenant.

"Take your time through the pre-engagement stage, too, Julia. Observe his family life. The way he treats his parents will likely be the way that he'll treat you. Can he hold down a job? Does he responsibly manage his money? Do you both want the same things out of life? Does he treat you like a treasure? Or are you just a possession? Are your wants and needs important to him? Or is the whole relationship geared only toward what he wants?

"You should find these things out before you commit to marry him. Don't get too critical, though. Nobody is perfect. Just decide for yourself whether the flaws you see are ones you can live with for a lifetime. There are no guarantees that things will change after you're married.

"Eventually, you'll know whether or not God has put you two together, and if so, you can confidently get engaged. This stage is great fun, Julia, because you've already done the hard work of making sure you are matched up with the right person. Now you can spend the next season joyfully getting ready for your life together.

"I'm sure that you're going to be working through some painful feelings and memories for a while now that your relationship with Jay is over. I know that you're hurting right now, Julia, and I really can't do much to help ease your pain. Only God and time will do that for you.

"Experiencing pain is unavoidable in life. But I can promise you one thing: the pain that you experience by waiting for God to bring your husband to you will vanish the moment you meet him. Then you'll be able to start your relationship with him without a lot of emotional problems. But if you try to make things happen prematurely, you're in for some major disappointments."

"I learned that the hard way with Jay," I admitted.

"Too bad more people haven't. Many people want to jump right from the discovery stage, where everything is new and exciting, directly into the intimacy stage, the one God designed for married couples to enjoy, one of sexual love and emotional transparency. Unfortunately, a lot of people ignore all the important stages between discovery and intimacy. They sleep with people they don't even know, not understanding why God wants them to save the sexual relationship for marriage. They don't realize the cost of what they're doing until the damage is already done—until they have an STD or an unwanted pregnancy or have experienced the rejection and emotional problems that sometimes come from a relationship that didn't work out."

My mom glanced down at her notebook. "We were going to look for a common thread in all your reasons for moving into the sorority house. After our talk, do you know what it was?"

"Not really…"

"I think I do. You lost your first love, Julia. Something became more important to you than your relationship with God, and you were willing to risk everything to get it. Nothing must ever be more valuable to you than Him, or it will become an idol. You'll worship that thing instead of God. You won't completely stop loving Him; you'll just love Him less. If this thread doesn't get cut, it'll weave itself into the fabric of your life. Eventually, something else you don't have will become *the thing* you desperately want. Then God will get pushed further back in your heart as you pursue it.

"We need to understand that everything in our earthly life is temporary; only our relationship with God is eternal and completely guaranteed. He will never leave us or forsake us. Never. Earthly relationships come and go. Even marriage is temporary; it will end eventually through death. But our relationship with God will always remain."

"That's beautiful, Mom," I answered, tearing up. "Why didn't you tell me about these things before? I'd been unhappy for so long about not having a boyfriend. If I'd understood all this, none of this mess with Jay would've happened!"

My mom was over on my side of the booth by now with her arm around me. "I didn't know you were hurting, Julia. You kept the pain you were feeling to yourself. When you were at home, you always seemed to be content. I assumed that you were happy and secure within your Christian life. I'm your mother, honey, not a mind reader. If you had confided in me, we could've had this talk before you left for school."

I looked up and smiled as she dried my tears with a nearby napkin. Then she dried a few of her own. "I'm just glad you're here, Mom, and we're having this girl talk now."

We'd been finished with our desserts and talking at our table for some time. No doubt the waitress wondered why we were taking so long, but it was our display of tears that attracted some inquiring eyes from her and several others in the room. That was the motivation we needed to gather up our things and leave. Embarrassed, we quickly paid our bill and left the restaurant. As we made our way to the car, my mom put her arm around my shoulder and said with a laugh, "Only women could end an evening with a good cry and consider it a night to remember."

Chapter 17

Looking Ahead

The next few days with my mother were great; all barriers to our relationship had been removed. It was like old times being together at the hotel. Fortunately, I breezed through my mid-week exams. Before I knew it, Friday afternoon had arrived, and I was sitting for my last final around three o' clock.

I had called Karen earlier and made arrangements to meet with my *rescue squad* after my exam. Karen, Gretchen, Gary, Kenny, and Fran were already at The Coffee Cup by the time I got there.

Everyone knew that I wouldn't be coming back the next fall, so we all exchanged addresses and phone numbers and promised to keep in touch. I tried to tell them how much I appreciated what they had done for me, but words couldn't express the gratitude in my heart. Somehow I felt they understood anyway.

Fran had finally accepted that marrying J.R. was not the right answer for her. She was going home to work things out with her family. The pastor at Gary's church had given him the name of a pregnancy assistance center in the city where Fran lived. Gary assured her that they would help her make the right decision for both her and the baby. She had agreed to contact them as soon as she got back.

Since her roommate was graduating, Karen invited Gretchen to room with her the coming fall. As it turned out, Karen would be her mentor, not me. I didn't feel qualified to disciple anyone at this stage in my life. I knew that between Karen and Gary, Gretchen would continue to grow in her relationship with Jesus.

Once the last goodbye was said, I returned to my car. As I unlocked my door, I noticed a note on my windshield. It was from Jay. It read:

Julia,

   Your dad said I couldn't see or talk to you again, but I couldn't let you go without asking you to forgive me. Honestly, I never meant to hurt you. I know now that you can't force someone to marry you. I'll never forget the love I felt for you, and I hope you'll find a guy one day that saved himself just for you.

                              Jay

As I read his note, the words *I never meant to hurt you* jumped out at me. It was a phrase that we had both used repeatedly in the last few months to the people we professed to love the most. I recognized it for what it was: an apology often used by selfish people. Perhaps it would be more appropriate to add, "I wanted my own way at your expense."

Not wanting to keep anything from Jay, I tore up the note and tossed it into a nearby trash can. Then I got into the car and drove to the library to return a few books I had borrowed. By the time I got back to the hotel room, my mom had already packed her bags for the trip home.

We went out for dinner again with the goal of being back early. I still needed to pack, and we wanted to get a good night's sleep before starting the long drive home. Talking and *laughing* at the restaurant this time, we returned a little later than planned.

Once we were back in our room, my mom put on her pajamas and climbed into bed to read. Meanwhile, I tackled my packing. I spent some time sorting through my school papers and threw away what I didn't need to keep. Then I folded my clothes and laid them neatly in my suitcase.

As I put in the last item, I looked over at my mother. She had fallen asleep with her glasses on, her Bible resting on her chest. This was a picture I had seen hundreds of times growing up. My mom kept a Bible on the table next to her bed and would often fall asleep after reading her passages for the night. My dad was usually the one to remove her glasses and Bible, place them on the nightstand, and turn out the light.

I sat there thinking about this amazing woman, how she unselfishly invested her life in her relationship with God and our family. Not once did she mention the pain, inconvenience, or expense I had caused her and my dad during the past week. My grandparents must have heard from the Lord when they named my mom Grace.

Now I understood that having a husband meant laying my life down to serve another person daily the way she had for my dad over the years. I also knew that I was nowhere near ready to be that kind of blessing in someone else's life. I needed to go home and learn to serve God first.

I was still meditating on the things my mom and I had discussed during our long talk at the restaurant. I remembered her saying that my detour into trouble was a direct result of losing Jesus as my first love. The more I thought about that, the more I realized I had never taken the time to develop Him as my first love. He was definitely one of my loves, but I couldn't honestly say that He'd been the first and most important.

This can sometimes be a problem for kids raised in Christian homes. We grow up going to church, learning about Jesus, and understanding our need for a savior. But once we receive Christ, we can easily think that is all there is to the relationship.

That's basically what happened with me. My experience with Jesus was based mostly on what I learned about Him from my parents and teachers at church. I read my Bible and prayed because I knew that's what all Christians should do. But I wasn't spending time with my Lord so I could know Him better.

Even though I'd wanted to serve God when I came to college, my love for Him hadn't been developed enough. Instead of relying on the Lord, I was focusing too much on people and things to meet my needs. I didn't realize then that a superficial relationship with Jesus could not sustain me in times of real temptation.

Your heart must be filled with genuine love, appreciation, and respect for God, for all that He is and all that He's done for you. And that only comes from spending time in His presence. As love and trust develop, you become more willing to sacrifice what you want in order to please Him. You come to understand that what He asks of you is always for your best anyway.

Obviously, I hadn't grown to that point yet. I saw that my devotional time with the Lord needed to become more personal. A desire for more of Him was already growing stronger within me. I purposed in my heart to take the time to make Jesus my first love when I returned home. I also needed to start *giving* into the relationships I had with my parents and church family. So far, I had only been taking from them.

There were two double beds in our hotel room, but I didn't want to sleep alone that night. I gently removed my mom's glasses and Bible and set them on the nearby table. Then I turned out the light and crawled into bed with her. She sensed my presence and opened up her arm so I could scoot in close beside her.

With her arm around me, I was reminded of when my father would be gone on a business trip and I would get to sleep in bed with her. I knew that in the morning, we would be going home and I'd have to start acting like an adult, but all I wanted at that moment was to snuggle with my mom and be her little girl for one more night.

My mom turned her head, kissed me on the forehead, and whispered, "Thank you, Father, for bringing our little girl's heart back home."

As I lay there, I was able to completely rest for the first time in months. I knew what I had done wrong and why, and there was an unwavering determination within me not to make the same mistakes again. My parents were close to me once more, and my secret life had finally come to a close. Deceit puts a heavy load of guilt on you mentally and emotionally—the more deceit, the greater the load. It was a relief to lay it down.

Just before falling asleep, something like a cleansing shower seemed to sweep through me. I smiled, realizing that I was experiencing the peace that accompanies a clear conscience. At last I was back to where I needed to be.

Even though my heart was badly bruised from my experiences at Tyler, with time and God's help, I would heal. My mistakes were behind me, and I was looking ahead, ready for the adventures that awaited me back home.

To be continued...

Meeting Mr. Right

Julia has learned a lot from her year at Tyler, but what happens when she returns home again? Go back with Julia as she reconnects with family and her best friend, Cassie. See how her growing relationship with God helps her to avoid more Mr. Wrongs, and how she helps girls who are facing issues like eating disorders, Internet predators, and sexual harassment. Watch as Julia finally meets her Mr. Right. You might be surprised who he turns out to be.

Finding You

Let's take a look at some of the characters in *Waiting for Mr. Right*. With which of them did **you** identify?

Julia

Perhaps you related to Julia. She had two loving Christian parents and had accepted Jesus at a young age. Yet when she went away to college, her life started to fall apart. Why?

Julia bought into the lie that the rules her parents had set up for her protection were way too strict, keeping her from having harmless fun. She forgot that her mom and dad had lived a lot longer than she had and were filled with a godly wisdom she hadn't acquired yet.

Just like Julia, the enemy of your soul wants you to think that the authorities in your life are withholding things from you for no good reason. If you don't resist those thoughts or talk to your parents about them, they will work on your mind until your desire to have or do something becomes stronger than your desire to obey what you know is right. At that point, you may be willing to do anything to get what you want, including hurting those around you who seem to get in the way.

Fortunately, one really bad experience opened Julia's eyes to what she was doing wrong and why. She was determined not to make the same foolish choices, and her heart was rededicated to truly living for God.

Gretchen

Maybe you're more like Gretchen. She represents the countless girls that are unaware of the potential dangers in life. Because they're ignorant of these dangers, they don't protect themselves against them. They often allow themselves to associate with the wrong people or be in unsupervised places, opening themselves up to situations where they can become deceived, used, or injured.

Gretchen said that Brad pressured her to have sex with him from the very beginning. She should have realized then that he didn't care one bit about her or what she wanted and needed; he only cared about himself. When she wouldn't willingly give him what he wanted, he just took it.

And when he did, a feeling of shame came over Gretchen. Even though she didn't choose to have sex with her boyfriend, the crime he committed against her brought a feeling of shame into her life all the same. In addition to that, she regretted how naive she had been. She probably asked herself a million times, "Why didn't I break up with Brad earlier? Why did I drink that glass of beer at the frat party? What was I thinking when I went up to his room?"

But of all the choices Gretchen made, the most foolish was her decision to keep on dating Brad. Now she knew what kind of man he was. Even so, she was deceived into thinking that her relationship with him was all she could hope for since she was no longer a virgin. What she failed to realize was that God loved her and He freely gives new beginnings to all who ask for them.

Because Gretchen didn't understand this, she continued to have sex with Brad after he forced himself on her. She was convinced that having Brad was better than nothing. But that's exactly what she got out of the relationship: nothing. Nothing positive, that is. All she received from him was an unexpected pregnancy, an unwanted abortion, and ongoing abuse.

Unlike many girls in her situation, Gretchen found a way out of her nightmare through a new and better relationship with God. Because she was able to receive His unconditional love and forgiveness, she was able to love and forgive herself. His love and acceptance gave her the strength to say *no* to Brad and *yes* to God. When we begin doing that, our choices start making today better and tomorrow what our heart desires.

When God forgave Gretchen, He gave her a new heart that had never been compromised. This would allow her to be married in the future and experience her first act of intimacy with her husband on their wedding night as a spiritually restored virgin. Only God can truly heal and replace what has been stolen or given away prematurely.

Though the memories of the past remain as a consequence of sin, the guilt connected with the past is forever removed. We are to use the memory of our mistakes to keep us on a better path and to help others who may still be walking in the dark.

Theresa

Before you can decide whether you see yourself as a Theresa, we need to take a closer look at her. Since she wasn't one of the main characters in the story, it would be easy to overlook her. Yet Theresa represents a lot of girls today.

The first question we might ask is *was she a Christian*? The first answer we might offer is *no* since she was so involved in a sorority known for partying. But wait a minute: Julia was definitely a Christian, and she had pledged there, too. So, what else do we know about Theresa?

She had a good heart, showing a lot of kindness and consideration toward others. She recruited new pledges, organized parties, freely loaned out her clothes, fixed girls' hair for special occasions, and remained positive and upbeat. Is it possible that Theresa did have a relationship with God, but like many people, didn't want anyone else to know about it?

Knowing God and talking about Him doesn't always make you popular with your peers. They treat you differently once they know. Some Christian girls decide that it's better to blend in and be more easily accepted and liked. The problem with blending in is that you soon become indistinguishable from unbelievers. Before you know it, you start talking and acting like them instead of like Jesus. You can never be an effective witness for Christ to them because they don't see that your life is any different from theirs.

Many of these girls take their need to be popular into their dating relationships, giving up their moral standards to please their boyfriends. These girls have a problem, though, once they have given in to sex: they can't bear for anyone to know. They are trying to live two different lives. They want to be popular with the people around them and, at the same time, be respected by other Christian believers.

These are the girls that will tell lies to cover up what they are doing. They would rather have an abortion than admit to a pregnancy. No one would know from outside appearances all the problems that compromise has caused them because they present a convincing façade when they are at church.

Often a girl like this will marry the man she has been having sex with, even though she knows she shouldn't. Maybe he's a weaker Christian than she is or not even a Christian at all. She convinces herself that everything will work out after they're married. She's afraid to put an end to the wrong relationship and trust God for someone better suited for her. She doesn't want to deal with the shame of having to tell another guy that she's already had sexual experiences.

In her heart, she knows what she's doing is wrong, and she therefore carries a heavy load of guilt. She rationalizes that if she marries her boyfriend, what they did sexually before marriage won't really matter since they ended up as man and wife. Unfortunately, pastors are constantly counseling Christian girls who have married men that do not sincerely love them, refuse to provide for them, or fail to assume their position as the spiritual leader of the home.

It's always wiser to admit your mistakes in the beginning, repent of them, and allow God to forgive you, heal you, and help change your future into a blessed one. It takes a lot of faith in God to get out of a wrong premarital relationship, start over again, and trust Him for the right man. But it takes even more faith to believe that once you're married, a husband who has no interest in God will ever want to change. Over time, some men do eventually surrender to God and allow Him to change them. Many never do.

Are you a Theresa-type Christian? If you're not sure, just ask yourself, "Do other people know that I'm a Christian? Am I willing to live a Christ-like life before them, even if I'm rejected for it?" If your answers are an honest *no*, you are definitely headed in that direction.

Fran

Fran came from a typical middle-class family that might have gone to church occasionally, but didn't have a genuine relationship with God. She represents people who base their lives on their feelings and what **they think** is right or wrong. They just do what they want (or what they think is good at the time) and then hope for the best. If it doesn't work out, they do whatever they can to escape the consequences that follow bad choices.

When Fran found out that she was pregnant, she wasn't sorry that she and J.R. had slept together. She only regretted getting pregnant and the problems that the pregnancy was causing her. Fran told Julia and Gretchen that she wanted J.R. to marry her. She didn't say that she loved him and wanted to build a future with him. She only said that he was partly responsible for her condition and therefore should be just as much a part of her solution.

In her conversation with the girls, she never once expressed a concern for the new life growing inside her body. She only talked about how the various options available would affect her own life. What about the way the baby would be affected?

Unfortunately, Fran didn't seem open to making a spiritual change in her life. Although Julia admittedly made some mistakes, she did care about her relationship with God and openly shared her faith with others. She also demonstrated a different set of values from other girls in the sorority. Fran had a chance to observe Julia while they roomed together. She knew firsthand that something was different about her roommate. She simply wasn't interested in the *Who* that made that difference. Fran was enjoying her life just as it was.

When Fran's pregnancy test read positive, she didn't turn to God for help; she turned to the same person that got her into trouble. When we do that, more trouble will surely follow. Gretchen tried to share with Fran her new Christian friends and her faith in God for a better future, but Fran wanted to work out a plan to fix things herself.

In the story, we learn that Fran decided against marrying J.R., but no decision had been reached regarding her baby. Which option do you think she chose? What would you have done? When Fran said, "...there's no good solution for me," she was expressing the frustration that comes when we don't do things the way God designed. There are always negative circumstances that follow, ones that hurt us and also cause hardships for others.

Some of the Frans of this world surrender to God in the midst of crisis and experience new life. Unfortunately, many of them do not.

Carrie, Lindsay, and Abby

The story didn't go into much detail about the lives of the three girls in the sorority that helped outfit Julia for the dance. These young women illustrate the people that we know by association but never take the time to really know. A girl can look confident and well adjusted on the outside while suffering miserably on the inside.

We would be amazed at the number of girls who have endured unhappy lives. Many have been raised in dysfunctional homes where the parents were immature and abusive, where divorce split the family apart, or where substance abuse was a daily problem.

There are so many different kinds of family backgrounds that it would be impossible to list them all. Yet all people have one thing in common: everyone is looking for unconditional love and acceptance. We try to get it from others, but

they can't give it to us. They don't have it. They
need it just as badly as we do. That's why a personal relationship with God is the only way to fill
that need in everyone's life. He alone is capable of
loving us unconditionally and accepting us completely. He's also the only one who can fully heal
us of past hurts and disappointments.

Karen

We saved Karen for last. Did you identify with
her? Karen's character is a good model and a great
encouragement. The story didn't say when Karen
had accepted Christ herself. The truth is, it didn't
matter. What did matter was the level of commitment she lived out once she had become a Christian.

While she was away from home and at college, Karen attended church regularly. She also put
herself under the accountability of her Bible study
group. Karen used her time at school to apply herself to her studies, apparently aware of the high
costs attached to getting her degree. She seemed
grateful to be in college and showed mature responsibility in the way she managed her schedule.
When Karen had free time, she spent it with her
Christian friends, and they actively shared the
Gospel with people they knew in their classes and
dorms.

You never once heard Karen complain about not having a boyfriend of her own. She was no different than any other girl on campus. She was probably just as excited to meet the man of her dreams. So why wasn't she frustrated like others? Is it possible that Karen had learned the secret to waiting for Mr. Right?

Karen wasn't seeking a boyfriend; she was seeking God. She was taking this season of her life to discover exactly who she was in Christ, her gifts, her callings, to find the plan of God for her life. She was excited to meet the man she would marry, but until she did, there was a lot to do for others. When you're thinking more about others, you don't have as much time to think about yourself. When you don't spend all of your time thinking about yourself, time has a way of speeding by.

God was preparing Karen to be a godly wife. Her future husband probably had schooling to complete, and so did she. Karen understood that God not only knew who was a good match for her, He knew when and where meeting her guy needed to take place. She trusted the Lord, not herself, to make it happen.

When you are tempted to be impatient or discontented with God's timing, feed on Scriptures about His faithfulness. Meditating on them will help to remind you of who God is, what He has already graciously done for you, and what He has promised to provide for you. As you seek Him with an open, grateful heart, your trust in Him will be strengthened, helping you to wait for what you want with an unwavering confidence that He will not disappoint you. And you will be able to enjoy life as you take on all the other God-adventures your Father has planned for you along the way.

Epilogue

As you read this book, did you think about your own spiritual life? Did you already know that God loves you and wants to be close to you—or did the relationship that Julia and her friends had with God seem strange or unattainable? Maybe no one has told you before how much you mean to God.

The Bible says in John 3:16-18: *God loved the people of this world so much that he gave his only Son, so that everyone who has faith in him will have eternal life and never really die. God did not send his Son into the world to condemn its people. He sent him to save them! No one who has faith in God's Son will be condemned. But everyone who doesn't have faith in him has already been condemned for not having faith in God's only Son.* (Contemporary English Version)

These verses tell us that God wants *everyone* to be in His family. Yet not everyone will be. We are all born with a sinful nature that separates us from a Holy God—and a sin debt that is too great for anyone to pay. That's why Jesus paid that debt for us on the cross. He paid what we could not. And now we have access to God the Father once again. All that remains is our choice to accept or reject His offer of salvation.

So, if you have never accepted Jesus as your Savior and Lord, you have a decision to make. Ask yourself: *Do I want to run my own life, miss heaven, and experience less than God's best for me right now? Or do I want to receive what Christ did for me and allow God to direct my life from this day forward, letting Him heal my past hurts and design a better future for me?* This choice is yours to make.

If you've already given your life to Jesus and received Him as *Savior*, you have His promise of eternal life in heaven. But it is important to make Christ the *Lord* of your life as well. When Jesus is your Lord, you seek God's will for your life, taking the time to pray, read the Bible, and then *do* what He tells you (to the best of your ability). As you honor God in this way, you will remain under the protective umbrella of His truth and provision. And you will experience the abundant blessings that come through simple faith, trust, and obedience. If you resist this part, however, you will miss out on much of God's best for your life.

How to Receive Jesus as Savior and Lord

If you have never given your life to the Lord but would like to, He is ready and willing to receive you. If you will pray this prayer from your heart, He will give you a new heart that wants to love and serve Him.

> *Heavenly Father, I come to you in Jesus' name and ask You to forgive me for the things I have done wrong and for wanting to live life my own way. Right now I invite Jesus to come into my heart and take control of my life. I believe that He died on the cross to pay for my sins: past, present and future. I believe that He was raised from the dead and will welcome me in heaven when my earthly life is over. Please help me to live for You and for others. I believe You have heard my prayer and that I have been born of Your Spirit. I confess Jesus as my Lord and Savior, and I am now a Christian, one who follows Christ.*

If you have prayed this prayer for the first time or are rededicating your life to the Lord, you need to find a church that teaches the Bible and will help you grow in your relationship with God. You won't be able to reach your full potential without the help of other Christians.

Learn from Julia. She went to church but didn't make the effort to get to know God for herself. The best way to do that is to set aside time to study your Bible and pray. Journaling is another way to connect with God as you record your thoughts and prayers. Over time you can see how you've grown and how God continues to take care of you.

From the Author

Now that our children are both happily married and raising their families, it's time for me to invest in spiritual daughters. I have a passion to help young girls make better choices and avoid the unnecessary heartbreaks that follow costly mistakes. I'm a firm believer that an ounce of prevention is worth a pound of cure.

I want to see the day when premarital sexual activity and pregnancies, abortions, and unhappy marriages are all but non-existent in the Body of Christ. The only way I know to see that accomplished is by offering the truth of God's Word to each of our girls and believing that they will have a willingness to receive it.

The entire **MR. RIGHT SERIES** was written in a story format to allow our Heavenly Father to reach out to His daughters everywhere, to communicate His love and acceptance to them in a way they could easily relate to and understand. He is waiting to bless and protect every girl or woman that will say *yes* to His offer to direct her life. As you are reading this, my prayer is that ***you*** will be one of them.

Credits

Contemporary English Version of the Bible:
Copyright © 1995 by American Bible Society
Found on biblegateway.com

**Unplanned Pregnancy Assistance Centers and
Pre and Post Abortion counseling, etc.:**
www.optionline.org   (800-395-HELP)

Order Information

To obtain additional copies of
Waiting for Mr. Right,
order online at:

www.MrRightSeries.com

Orders usually ship within 24 hours.

For discounts on bulk orders, send inquiries to:

precourtbooks@gmail.com

Waiting for Mr. Right is Book 1 of the
Mr. Right Series

For information regarding Books 2 and 3:
Meeting Mr. Right
Marrying Mr. Right

check online at:

www.MrRightSeries.com

About the Book

JULIA DUNCAN arrives at Tyler University with high hopes of meeting someone: a handsome prince who will sweep her off her feet. Eventually, Julia *does* find a boyfriend who seems to be Mr. Right. But time reveals that he is just the opposite, and her romantic dream suddenly becomes a nightmare. Watch how living a lie takes Julia further and further away from the life she wants to live. Get to know her friends on campus and see how they deal with issues like unwanted pregnancies, abusive boyfriends, and being a true friend. Witness how one nugget of truth saves Julia's life and puts her back on track to experience God's very best.

About the Author

BARBARA PRECOURT resides in Valparaiso, Indiana with her husband, Roger. Her life is centered in her family, her church, and her husband's insurance agency. Her writing reflects over thirty years of Bible study and teaching.

After seeing her own daughter happily married, Barbara wrote this novel to help other young women wait for their Mr. Right and avoid all the Mr. Wrongs who will no doubt pursue them.

ISBN 978-160844-032-0

51395

9 781608 440320

READ THE NEXT TWO
BOOKS IN THE SERIES:

Meeting Mr. Right
Marrying Mr. Right